SPEECH SOUND INTERVENTIONS

30 GROUP INTERVENTIONS TO DEVELOP SECURE SPEECH AND PHONICS FOUNDATIONS

LIZ SPOONER
JACQUI WOODCOCK

BLOOMSBURY EDUCATION
LONDON OXFORD NEW YORK NEW DELHI SYDNEY

BLOOMSBURY EDUCATION
Bloomsbury Publishing Plc
50 Bedford Square, London WC1B 3DP, UK
Bloomsbury Publishing Ireland Limited
29 Earlsfort Terrace, Dublin 2, D02 AY28, Ireland

BLOOMSBURY, BLOOMSBURY EDUCATION and the Diana logo are trademarks
of Bloomsbury Publishing Plc

First published in Great Britain, 2026 by Bloomsbury Publishing Plc
This edition published in Great Britain, 2026 by Bloomsbury Publishing Plc

Text copyright © Liz Spooner and Jacqui Woodcock, 2026

Liz Spooner and Jacqui Woodcock have asserted their rights under the Copyright,
Designs and Patents Act, 1988, to be identified as Authors of this work

Bloomsbury Publishing Plc does not have any control over, or responsibility for, any third-party websites referred to or in this book. All internet addresses given in this book were correct at the time of going to press. The author and publisher regret any inconvenience caused if addresses have changed or sites have ceased to exist, but can accept no responsibility for any such changes

Cover images © iStock: monkeybusinessimages, Shutterstock: GagliardiPhotography,
KK Tan, monkeybusinessimages, Savicic
Resource images © Helen Eurell

All rights reserved. This publication may be photocopied solely for use in the educational establishment for which it was purchased but otherwise no part of this publication may be reproduced or transmitted in any form, electronic or mechanical, including photocopying, recording or by means of any information storage or retrieval system without prior permission in writing from the publishers. No part of this publication may be used or reproduced in any way for the training, development or operation of artificial intelligence (AI) technologies, including generative AI technologies. The rights holders expressly reserve this publication from the text and data mining exception as per Article 4(3) of the
Digital Single Market Directive (EU) 2019/790.

A catalogue record for this book is available from the British Library

ISBN: PB: 978-1-80199-749-2; ePub: 978-1-80199-747-8

2 4 6 8 10 9 7 5 3 1 (paperback)

Cover design by Amanda Carroll
Text design by Jeni Child

Printed and bound in the UK by Ashford Colour Ltd

To find out more about our authors and books visit www.bloomsbury.com
and sign up for our newsletters
For product safety related questions contact productsafety@bloomsbury.com

CONTENTS

SECTION 1: RUNNING THIS INTERVENTION

1. About this intervention 4
2. Typical speech sound development 7
3. How to help children make speech sounds 9
4. The structure of the sessions 12

SECTION 2: WEEKLY SESSIONS

Week 1 14
Week 2 16
Week 3 18
Week 4 20
Week 5 22
Week 6 24
Week 7 26
Week 8 28
Week 9 30
Week 10 32
Week 11 34
Week 12 36
Week 13 38
Week 14 40
Week 15 42
Week 16 44
Week 17 46
Week 18 48
Week 19 50
Week 20 52
Week 21 54
Week 22 56
Week 23 58
Week 24 60
Week 25 62
Week 26 64
Week 27 66
Week 28 68
Week 29 70
Week 30 72

SECTION 3: PHOTOCOPIABLE ACTIVITY RESOURCES

1. Syllable clap cards 74
2. Animal noises cards 75
3. Rhyming rule card 76
4. Rhyming pictures 77
5. Sequencing caterpillar cards 85
6. Picnic rhyming game 88
7. Syllable picture cards 89
8. Vowel cards 93
9. Animal picnic game cards 94
10. Compound word picture cards 96
11. Syllable-blending picture cards 98
12. Yes/no cards 100
13. VC word lists 101
14. Initial sound pictures 102
15. Minimal pair pictures 108
16. Word takeaway lists 110
17. Rhyme judgement pictures 111
18. Final sound pictures 115
19. Word chain lists 119
20. Win the rhyme word lists 120
21. Same/different cue card 121
22. Same/different judgement word lists 122
23. Game board 123
24. Syllable dominoes 124
25. Is my sound in the word? 128
26. Add a syllable step up pictures 129
27. Where in the word? 130
28. Real and nonsense words 131
29. Final sound/no final sound picture cards 132
30. Tricky syllable picture cards 135
31. CCVC word lists 136
32. One and two cards 137
33. 'l' blend minimal pairs cards 138
34. What's the new word? 141
35. People picnic game cards 142
36. 's' blend minimal pairs cards 145
37. Add a syllable, make a word 147
38. Final blend minimal pairs cards 149
39. Anchor words 152
40. Final blend word list (CVCC words) .. 155
41. Rhyme workshop cards 156
42. Catch me doing it! 158
43. Consonant blends 159

1

ABOUT THIS INTERVENTION

Who is this intervention for?

Up to 25% of children in the UK start school without being able to accurately use all of the speech sounds we need to communicate (McFaul et al., 2022). This can make it harder for them to talk to their friends and make themselves understood to adults, and crucially, it can affect their progress in phonics.

Most children who have speech sound difficulties are able to make the sounds they need but find it hard to use them accurately in words because of difficulties with their phonological processing. Phonological processing is 'the ability to manipulate and make judgements about the sounds that make up spoken words' (Stackhouse and Wells, 1997). Robust phonological processing is the foundation that helps children both to use speech sounds accurately and also develop phonics skills successfully.

This intervention is designed to target the phonological processing skills that children need for accurate speech sound use, using structured incremental activities which have been designed to be delivered over an academic year.

Who to include

Children with speech sound delay

This can include children who are already known to a Speech and Language Therapist or who are awaiting an appointment. The activities in the intervention will complement specific targets that have been set for children and will provide additional opportunities for them to practise alongside their peers.

This resource can also be used as a targeted intervention as part of the graduated response to support children once you have identified a concern with speech sounds. See 'When to refer to Speech and Language Therapy'.

Children who need additional support with phonics

Children with no obvious speech sound difficulties but who need additional support to blend and segment sounds can also be included, as they will benefit from the additional practice with the skills that the intervention activities provide.

Are they ready?

Some children with speech sound difficulties are not yet developmentally ready to access phonological processing intervention and may need to develop other skills first. The following flowchart will help you to check that the children you select for your group will be ready to make progress.

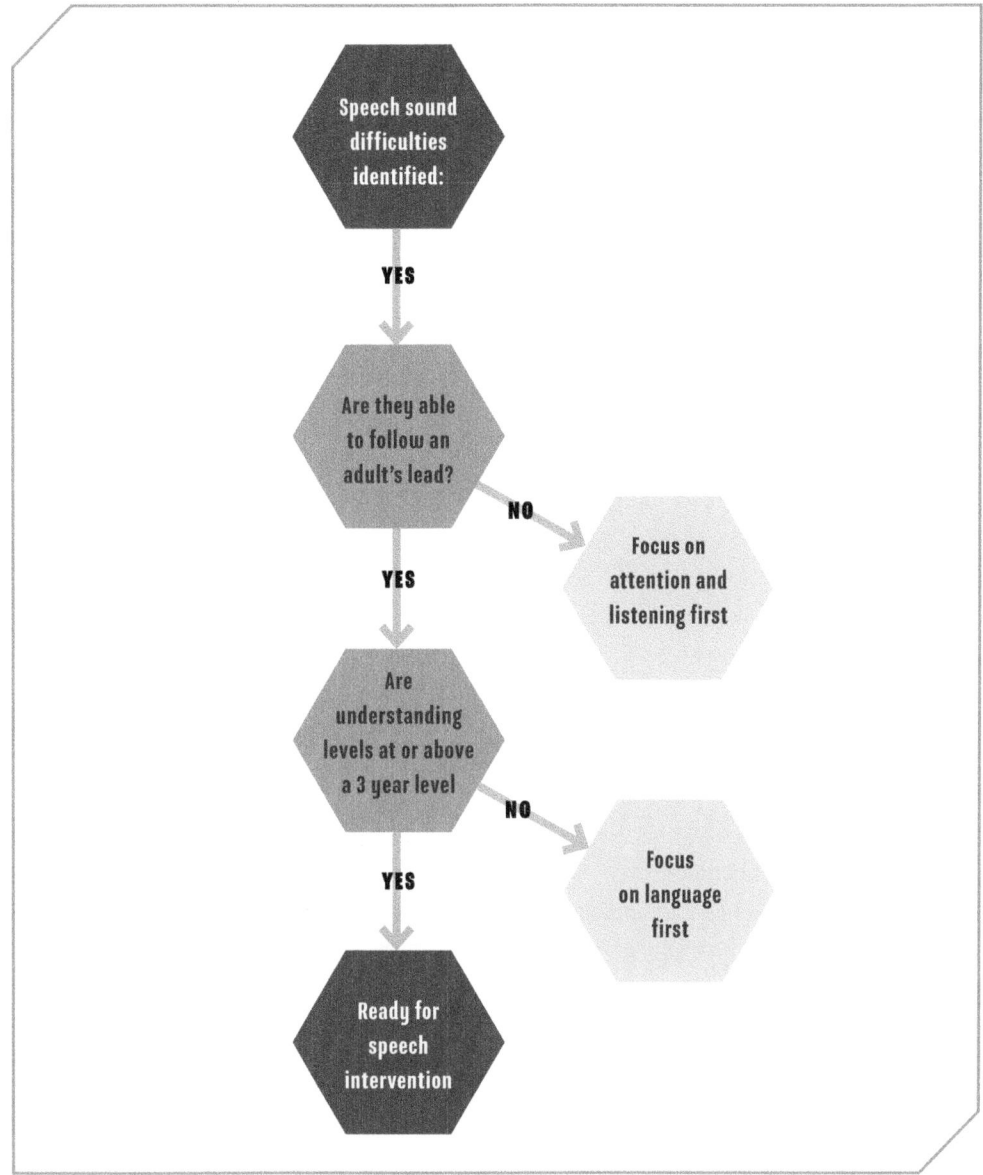

How to deliver the intervention

This targeted intervention has 30 sessions designed to be delivered over the course of an academic year. We recognise that the capacity to deliver interventions in school is always under pressure, so these sessions can be delivered flexibly.

- Each session can be delivered weekly (20 – 30 minutes).
- Alternatively, shorter sessions can be delivered twice weekly (10 – 15 minutes), including two activities each time.

How many children to include

Creating a group of 4 – 6 children enables everyone to have an opportunity to take part.

The intervention sessions can be delivered to smaller groups or individually if this would be more appropriate for the needs of the children.

Where to deliver the intervention

The intervention activities require children to listen carefully to sounds and so a quiet environment where background noise is limited as much as possible will really help them. Sitting on chairs round a table will help children to focus and will enable them to see and use resources appropriately.

Using step up and step down

You can include children in your group who are working at different levels for different skills. Each activity has a step up and a step down suggestion to help you differentiate for the different needs of the children in your group.

The step up is provided to help children make quick progress within a session if possible. You can use the step up with all children if everyone is confident with the activity or just to provide an extra level of challenge for specific children who are progressing quickly.

The step down is provided to ensure children who need additional support can still access the activity. Again this can be used for the whole group if needed or just to support an individual child.

Resources

All of the resources needed to deliver the intervention are included within Section 3 and can also be downloaded from bloomsbury.pub/speech-sound-interventions. The resources you will need are indicated within each session plan. It will help smooth delivery of the intervention if all of the resources are prepared in advance.

TYPICAL SPEECH SOUND DEVELOPMENT

Typical development of sounds

Young children gradually learn to use new sounds during their pre-school years. Some sounds typically develop earlier than others. By the time a child starts school at 4-5 years old, they will usually be able to use most sounds accurately and they should be easy for most people to understand.

The typical pattern for the development of English sounds is shown below:

Age	Sounds
3 years	p, b, t, d, k, g, m, n, ng, f, h, y, w
4 years	v, s, z, sh, ch, l
5 years	r, zh (as in 'treasure') th (voiced as in 'the')
6 years	th (voiceless as in 'thumb')

(McCleod & Crowe, 2018)

As most young children learn new sounds in a predictable way, we often hear familiar patterns in the errors that they make. These are some of the patterns you may hear:

Fronting
Back of the mouth sounds 'ck' and 'g' are made at the front of the mouth to become 't' and 'd' e.g. 'car' would be 'tar' and 'game' would be 'dame'.

Stopping
Long sounds such as 's'; 'f'; 'sh' are replaced by short sounds such as 'd' or 'b'. e.g. 'fire' might be 'bire' or 'sunny' might be 'dunny'.

Gliding
There are four 'glide' sounds which are made by sliding our tongue or lips. These are 'r'; 'w'; 'l' and 'y'. These are typically later sounds to develop and many reception-age children will not be using them consistently yet. Gliding is when children confuse two of these sounds; typically 'r' becomes 'w' and 'l' becomes 'y' or 'w'.

Final consonant deletion
The last sound is missed out e.g. 'bag' would be 'ba'.

Blend reduction
The child reduces a consonant blend to just one sound e.g. 'snake' becomes 'nake' and 'flower' might be 'fower'.

Weak syllable deletion
Most words in English have the stress on the first syllable. Occasionally the stress is on the second syllable and this can make it harder for children to hear and say the first part of the word which means they leave it out e.g. they might say 'computer' as 'puter' or banana' as 'nana'.

Voicing
Quiet voiceless sounds are replaced by the equivalent voiced sound. E.g 'pig' might be 'big' or 'cat' might be 'gat'. Children usually grow out of this before they start school.

When to refer to Speech and Language Therapy
When deciding whether to make a referral, it is helpful to consider the following factors. Consider a referral if:
- a child of Reception age or above is having consistent difficulties making themselves understood.
- you can hear them using more than one of the typical development processes discussed above.
- they are using unusual processes other than the typical developmental processes listed. For example, if they 'back' sounds to 'ck' and 'g' e.g. 'daddy' is 'gaggy'.
- they replace lots of different consonants with the same sound – for example, if they use 'd' for many sounds so that 'five' is 'dive'; 'soap' is 'doap' and 'table' is 'dable'.
- they make inconsistent incorrect substitutions e.g. 'zip' becomes 'dip' but 'buzz' becomes 'bug'.
- vowels are inaccurate e.g. 'night' is said as 'nart' or 'same' is 'sem'.

If a child is just showing one developmental process and they are generally intelligible then it might be appropriate to use this intervention as part of the graduated response, with a referral being made if their difficulties do not fully resolve.

This intervention will support all children with speech sound difficulties and referred and non-referred children can all be included in the same group.

HOW TO HELP CHILDREN MAKE SPEECH SOUNDS

Ways to help children make speech sounds

Most children with speech sound difficulties can copy a sound when an adult makes it for them. However, some children need a little extra practice to learn how to articulate some of the trickier sounds.

General principles

- Make sure they can see your face so they can see how you are making the sounds.
- Make sure the environment is as quiet as possible so they can hear the sound clearly.
- Using a mirror (or a tablet with the video flipped) will enable the child to see as well as feel what they are doing.
- Once a child has successfully made a new sound, it is helpful to practise it as many times as possible in isolation so that they get very familiar with how it feels to say that sound and can make it more easily in future.
- Many sounds in English are made in almost the same way with the only difference being whether the vocal cords are used or not. You can feel this yourself if you put your fingers on the front of your neck and make a long 'ss' sound. If you then turn this into a 'zz' sound you will feel the vibration of your vocal cords which are needed for this sound. You can try this with other pairs of sounds such as f/v; t/d; ck/g; p/b etc. For this reason these sounds are grouped together in the table below. Try the voiceless sound first and once they have learned how to make that, turn it into the voiced one.

Ideas for teaching specific sounds

Sounds	What to try:
p & b	◯ Show them how to put their lips together.
	◯ Encourage them to make a 'popping' sound.

t & d	○ Show them how to put their tongue just behind their top teeth.
	○ Practise making your tongue 'jump' there to make a short sound.
	○ If they find this hard, they can try making a 't' sound much further forward with their tongue on their teeth or lips so they get the idea of making it at the front of their mouths. Once they can do this you can shape it by gradually moving it back to the right place behind their top teeth.
ck & g	○ Remind them that we make these sounds at the back of our mouths.
	○ Encourage them to open their mouths very wide and keep their mouth open while they make the sound right at the back.
	○ Asking them to look up to the ceiling while they make the sound can encourage their tongue to fall back into the right position.
	○ If they are still finding it tricky to make the sound then teaching them a new sound made in the same place can be helpful. For example, a long 'kkkkk' monster sound (e.g. the Scottish 'ch' in 'loch') can be easy for many children to learn. Once they can do this, you can shape it by gradually making it shorter.
f & v	○ Show them how to bite their bottom lip gently. A mirror can be really helpful for this sound.
	○ Once they have put their teeth in the right place, encourage them to blow gently.
	○ If children are finding it hard to put their teeth in the right place then visualisation can be a helpful strategy. Ask them to imagine they are eating ice cream and it is running down their chin and they have to catch it with their teeth. This can often help them achieve the right placement.
s & z	○ Show them how to put their tongue just behind their teeth and blow gently.
	○ Some children can make a 's' sound using a 't' as a jumping off point. Ask them to make a few 't' sounds and then make the last one extra long e.g. 't..t..t..sssss'
	○ If they are finding it hard to put their tongue in the right place then you can help them by asking them to copy a 'th' sound which many children find easier.

		○ Once they can do a 'th' consistently, you can shape this into a 'ss' by moving it slowly back so their tongue is behind their teeth again.
sh		○ This can be a tricky sound for lots of children to make. Using a mirror might help them see how to make the sound.
		○ Show them how to push their lips forwards and remind them that they do not need to use their tongue to make this sound – it can have a rest at the bottom of their mouth!
ch & j		○ These sounds are much easier to teach if children can already make a 'sh' sound so try that sound first.
		○ Once they can make a 'sh' sound consistently, you can shape this sound by gradually making it shorter and shorter.
		○ Some children can achieve a 'ch' sound if you ask them to 'freeze' while making a 'sh' sound and keep their mouth in the same place and letting all the air out quickly.
l		○ Explain when we write a 'l' sound our pencil starts at the top and goes all the way to the bottom and when we say a 'l' sound our tongue does the same thing. It has to go to our top teeth and all the way down to make a 'l'.
		○ If they are still finding it tricky then try making an 'ah' sound with their tongue sticking out. Continue to make the 'ah' as they gently close and open their mouth to produce a 'l' e.g. 'ah..l..ah'
r		○ Using a mirror will really help them to see how this sound is made.
		○ Explain that when we make a 'r' sound our bottom lip has to get very close to your top teeth and demonstrate this.
		○ Remind them that their bottom lip cannot get close their top lip or the sound will turn into a 'w'.
th		○ Remind them that we are allowed to put our tongue out when we make this sound.
		○ Practise sticking your tongue between your teeth and blowing the air out.

4

THE STRUCTURE OF THE SESSIONS

Activities in each session

Each session has one activity from each of the following sections.

 LISTEN FOR IT:

The activities in this section are designed to help children to hear the differences between sounds. Some sounds are just too similar for children to be able to hear the difference easily and they need opportunities to listen to them many times in a quiet environment.

These activities also help children to:

- hear the difference between their target sounds and the ones they replace them with.
- learn segmentation skills: the ability to break words apart in different ways. This is an essential skill children need for speech sound intervention but also for developing their literacy.
- practise these skills in small incremental achievable steps.

 CLAP IT:

The activities in this section aim to help children listen to a word and break it down into syllables. Helping children to use the right number of syllables when saying a word is the fastest way to improve the intelligibility of their talking.

These activities also help children to:

- store the sounds in words accurately.
- learn, remember and use new vocabulary.

SAY IT:

This section has activities which are designed to help children use sounds accurately in words.

These activities will help children to:

- develop the ability to self-monitor how they are saying sounds in words.
- practise using sounds straight after judgement tasks, where they have been listening for them.
- practise using target sounds in new or nonsense words. It is often easier for children to use sounds accurately in new words, rather than changing how they say words which they have already learned incorrectly.

 RHYME IT:

The activities in this section are designed to help children hear and identify rhyming patterns between words.

These activities will help children to:

- develop speech sound accuracy for vowels and final sounds.
- generalise progress across words that rhyme.
- identify sound patterns that will support their spelling skills.

WEEK 1

LISTEN FOR IT: MATCHING MUSICAL INSTRUMENTS

What you need:
- Two sets of matching musical instruments or a set of musical instruments and matching photographs

- Let each child have a turn at playing each instrument first.
- Explain to the children that you are going to play one of the instruments and they have to find one that makes the same sound.
- On the first turn for each child, play the instrument so the child can see and ask the child to find the matching instrument or photo.
- When the children can do this consistently, explain that you are going to make the game harder by hiding the instrument while you play it, so they just have to listen.
- Direct the children to takes turns at listening to a hidden instrument and finding the matching instrument or photo.

Step down
- Choose just two instruments that sound quite different, such as bells and a shaker.

Step up
- Increase the number of instruments to choose from.
- Choose instruments that sound more similar e.g. two different shakers.

CLAP IT: CLAP YOUR NAME

What you need:
- Syllable clap cards (Resource 1)

- Show the children the syllable clap cards and explain that everyone has claps in their name. Some people have a short name with just one clap, e.g. Jack (one syllable), and some people might have a long name with lots of claps, e.g. Amelia (four syllables).
- Explain that you are going to clap everyone's name to find out how many claps it has.
- Start by demonstrating with your own name.
- Ask everyone to get their hands ready to clap each time, and remember to say 'ready, steady, go' so that everyone claps at the same time.
- Clap out your name, e.g. 'Miss John – son'.
- Say your name again and count on your fingers as you say each syllable, so children can see as well as hear how many syllables are in the name.
- Try this again, with the children saying and clapping your name.
- Ask the children to find the right syllable clap card for your name, and check it by saying the name as you touch each clap on the card.
- Give each child a turn to clap their own name in the same way, to decide how many claps they have.

Step down
- Clap each child's name together as a group, including you as the adult.

Step up
- Once the children have identified how many claps are in their names, play a game in which they have to listen for an action. Give instructions such as: 'If you have two claps in your name, stand up' or 'If you have three claps in your name, put your finger on your nose'.

SAY IT: ANIMAL SOUNDS

What you need:
- Animal noises cards (Resource 2)
- A second set of animal noises cards (Resource 2) for the step down activity

Using symbolic noises, such as animal sounds, is a useful introduction to teaching children that a picture or symbol can represent a sound.

- Show the children the animal noises cards and check that they are familiar with the animals and what sounds they make.
- Give each child a card and explain that they have to listen for their animal sound. When they hear it, they must stand up and then sit down again.
- Make the animals' sounds, ensuring that you make every sound more than once and use a random sequence.
- When you are confident that the children know the sound that goes with each picture, change the game so that, instead of making the sound yourself, you show the group the picture and the person with that animal has to stand up, make the sound and sit down again.

Step down
○ Start by showing the pictures while you make the sounds.

Step up
○ Choose a child to be the 'teacher' so they make the sounds for everyone else.

RHYME IT: WIN THE PICTURE

What you need:
- Rhyming rule card (Resource 3)
- Rhyming pictures (Resource 4)

- Using the rhyming rule card, explain the rule about rhyming words: the first sound is different and the rest of the word sounds the same.
- Explain that you have lots of pictures and you are going to see if the children can win them from you by guessing what they are. You are not going to say the name of the thing in the picture, but you are going to give them two clues. They have to listen to your clues and see whether they can guess what your picture is.
- Choose one of the rhyming picture cards, but don't let the children see what it is. Read out the two clues for that picture and see who can guess what your picture is, e.g. 'I've got something that shines in the sky and it rhymes with "bun".'
- If a child guesses correctly, give them the picture and say the two words a few times so they can really hear the rhyme pattern, e.g. 'Yes, bun… sun… bun… sun. The first sound is different but the rest is the same.'

Step down
○ Give the children a choice of two answers, e.g. 'It shines in the sky and rhymes with "bun" – is it a rocket or is it a sun?'

Step up
○ Try some of the pictures again, but this time give only the rhyming clue, e.g. 'What was the picture that rhymed with "sock"?'

WEEK 2

LISTEN FOR IT: SEQUENCING MUSICAL INSTRUMENTS ACTIVITY ONE

What you need:
- Sequencing caterpillar (Resource 5): two segments
- Sets of matching musical instruments, or sets of musical instruments and matching photographs: two instruments to be used during each turn

- Show the children the sequencing caterpillar.
- Explain that you are going to play the instrument game again but that this time it is going to be even trickier: the children have to listen for two sounds. The first instrument they hear will be placed on the caterpillar's head and the second one they hear will go on his body.
- Choose a child to have the first turn and put two different instruments (or photos) in front of them.
- Hiding them, play the matching instruments in sequence. Remind the child to wait until they have heard both instruments, and then to put their matching instruments on the caterpillar in the correct order.
- Bring your instruments out in the correct order so the child can see whether they were correct.

Step down
○ Comment on what you are doing as you play the sequence, e.g. 'First bells and next shaker.'

Step up
○ Use two instruments that sound similar.
○ Play them for shorter amounts of time.

CLAP IT: MYSTERY BAG CLAPPING

What you need:
- Syllable clap cards (Resource 1)
- Small objects in a bag, such as pretend food and toy vehicles

- Remind the children that, in the last session (from week 1), they were thinking about the numbers of claps in different words.
- Explain that you have lots of things in your bag and they are all mixed up; the children are going to help you sort them out by matching each of them to the right syllable clap card.
- Give each child a turn to choose an object from the bag and say what it is. On each child's first turn, support them by clapping out the word as a group.
- Ask everyone to get their hands ready to clap, and remember to say 'ready, steady, go' so that everyone claps at the same time as you clap the word together, e.g. 'bu – tter – fly'.
- Say the word again and count on your fingers as you say each syllable so children can see as well as hear how many syllables are in it.
- Ask the children to find the right syllable clap card for the word, and check it by saying the word as you touch each clap on the card.
- Once the children are confident with the activity, challenge each child to choose an object from the bag and clap its name independently.

Step down
○ Choose objects with only one or two syllables in their name, such as trains, lorries, cars and tractors.

Step up
○ Choose objects with a wide range of syllable numbers, such as lorries, cars, tractors, aeroplanes and helicopters.

SAY IT: SEQUENCING ANIMAL NOISES

What you need:
For the 'Step up' activity (resources per child):
- Sequencing caterpillar (Resource 5): two segments
- Animal noises cards (Resource 2)

- Remind the children about the sequencing caterpillar (from this week's listen for it activity).
- Explain that you are going to put two pictures on the caterpillar and see if the children can 'read' the sounds they make.
- Remind the children that the first sound is always on the caterpillar's head.
- Assemble a sequence of two animal pictures on the caterpillar, and see if the group can make the sounds in the right order.
- Repeat this, making a different sequence each time, so that every child has a turn.

Step down
- Reduce the number of animal noise cards.

Step up
- Challenge each child to make a secret sequence for the other children and 'read' it to them to make on their own caterpillar cards.

RHYME IT: PICNIC RHYMES

What you need:
- Rhyming rule card (Resource 3)
- Picnic rhyming game (Resource 6)
- A lunch box

Rhyme can be a challenging concept. Introducing it with a rhyming string gives children lots of opportunities to hear the sound sequence that makes up the rhyme.

- Explain that you are going to pack a picnic with the picnic rhyming cards, but you can only put things in that rhyme.
- Using the rhyming rule card, remind the children of the rule about rhyming words: the first sound is different and the rest of word sounds the same.
- Choose a picnic rhyme card, hide it and say the matching rhyming clue for the group.
- Once the children have guessed the picnic item, say the rhyme again for them and put the card in the lunch box.

Step down
- Add some extra rhymes and more information about it the item on a card: for example, 'papple... dapple... bapple... gapple... I think we will take a juicy... [pause]. It's something that grows on a tree.'

Step up
- Instead of working as a group, give children turns individually to listen to the rhyming clue.

WEEK 3

LISTEN FOR IT: SEQUENCING MUSICAL INSTRUMENTS ACTIVITY TWO

What you need:
- Sequencing caterpillar (Resource 5): two segments
- Sets of three matching musical instruments or sets of three musical instruments and their matching photographs: one set to be used during each turn

- Explain that you are going to play the instrument game again (from week 2) but this time it is going to be even trickier: the children still have to listen for two sounds, they will now have *three* different instruments to choose from when identifying them.
- Remind the children about the sequencing caterpillar (from week 2): the first instrument they hear will still go on the caterpillar's head and the second one they hear will go on his body.
- Choose a child to have the first turn and put the three matching instruments (or photos) in front of them.
- Hiding them, play two of the instruments in sequence. Remind the child to wait until they have heard both instruments, and then to put the matching instruments on the caterpillar in the correct order.
- Bring your instruments out in the correct order so the children can see whether they were correct.
- Give each child a turn, changing the sequence each time.

Step down
○ Reduce the choice back down to two instruments so the children have to think about only the right order.

Step up
○ Increase the choice of instruments.
○ Use instruments that sound similar.
○ Play them for shorter amounts of time.

CLAP IT: LISTENING FOR ONE OR THREE SYLLABLES: TRANSPORT

What you need:
- Syllable clap cards (Resource 1): one and three clap words
- Syllable picture cards (Resource 7): modes of transport with one or three syllables

- Explain that you have lots of pictures: some show modes of transport with just one clap in their name and some show modes of transport with three. The children are going to help you sort them out by matching each to the right syllable clap card.
- Put the pictures face down on the table and ask children to take it in turns to choose one and name it.
- Ask everyone to get their hands ready to clap, and remember to say 'ready, steady, go' so that everyone claps at the same time. Then clap the word together, e.g. 'ice – cream – van'.
- Say the word again and count on your fingers as you say each syllable so the children can see as well as hear how many syllables are in the word.
- Ask the children to match it to the right syllable clap card, and check it by saying the word as you touch each clap on the card.

Step down
○ Say and clap the word represented by the picture first, so the children can copy your model.

Step up
○ Instead of working as a group, give children turns individually to clap out each word.

SAY IT: VOWEL SOUNDS

What you need:
- Vowel cards (Resource 8)
- Sequencing caterpillar (Resource 5): two segments

- Show the children the three vowel picture cards and practise making the sounds.
- Show them one vowel at a time and see whether they can make the right sound.
- Explain that you are going to put two sounds on the sequencing caterpillar and that the children are then going to 'read' the sequence together.
- Remind them that the first sound is always on the caterpillar's head.
- Give each child a turn to 'read' the sounds on the caterpillar, changing the sequence each time.

Step down
- Reduce the choice to two possible vowels.
- If a particular child finds this activity challenging, let another read a sequence first and then give them the same sequence to read for themselves.

Step up
- Let the children take turns to make a sequence for themselves and then read it.

RHYME IT: ANIMAL PICNIC GAME

What you need:
- Animal picnic game cards (Resource 9)

- Show the children the animal picnic cards.
- Explain that the animals are going on a picnic but each of them only eats food that rhymes with its name. The food has got mixed up, and the children need to help by sorting it out.
- Put out all the food pictures, naming them with the children.
- Choose an animal and say its name.
- Choose two food pictures (including the one of the target rhyme) and say each food with the animal's name, allowing the children to hear whether they rhyme, e.g. 'Larry Lamb – what does he like? Lamb, cake, or Lamb, ham?'

Step down
- Choose the right food for the children, and use the opportunity to model the two rhyming words many times, e.g. 'Polly parrot likes the carrot.
Listen: parrot, carrot; parrot, carrot.'

Step up
- Instead of working as a group, give children turns individually to decide which rhyming food each animal wants to eat.
- Give the children a choice of three possible foods for each animal to eat.

WEEK 4

LISTEN FOR IT: LISTENING FOR COMPOUND WORDS ACTIVITY ONE

What you need:
- Sequencing caterpillar (Resource 5): two segments
- Compound word picture cards (Resource 10): set one and word list

- Check the children are familiar with what the compound word picture cards show.
- Explain that you are going to make some words on the caterpillar, but you are not going to use letters to do it: you are going to use pictures instead. Each word will be made up of two pictures. The first picture you will name goes on the caterpillar's head and the second goes on the caterpillar's tail.
- Take the first turn to make a compound word on the caterpillar, and read this together with the children, e.g. 'Pan, cake: pancake.'
- Say a new compound word (such as 'postman'), and ask a child to find the two pictures they need and sequence them on the caterpillar.
- When they have the right pictures in the right order, ask the children to 'read' the word together.

Step down
- If a child finds only the first picture, say the word again and leave a gap between the two word parts, e.g. 'post... man'.
- If a child chooses the right pictures but puts them in the wrong order (e.g. 'manpost'), 'read' the word together so they can hear that it does not sound right. Then ask the child to change the sequence to make the correct word.

Step up
- Challenge the children to change one picture to make a new word, e.g. they could change 'postman' to 'postbox'.

CLAP IT: LISTENING FOR ONE OR THREE SYLLABLES: MINIBEASTS

What you need:
- Syllable clap cards (Resource 1): one and three clap words
- Syllable picture cards (Resource 7): minibeasts with one or three syllables

- Explain that you have lots of pictures: some of them show things with just one clap in their name and some show things with three. The children are going to help you sort them out by matching each to the right syllable clap card.
- Put the pictures face down on the table and ask children to take it in turns to choose one and name it.
- Ask everyone to get their hands ready to clap, and remember to say 'ready, steady, go' so that everyone claps at the same time. Then clap the word together, e.g. 'bu – tter – fly'.
- Say the word again and count on your fingers as you say each syllable so the children can see as well as hear how many syllables are in the word.
- Ask the children to match the word to the right syllable clap card, and check it by saying the word as you touch each clap on the card.

Step down
- Say and clap the word represented by the picture first, so the children can copy your model.

Step up
- Instead of working as a group, give children turns individually to clap out each word.

SAY IT: 'READING' COMPOUND WORDS ACTIVITY ONE

What you need:
- Sequencing caterpillar (Resource 5): two segments
- Compound word picture cards (Resource 10): set one and word list

- Explain that you are going to make some words on the sequencing caterpillar, but again you are going to use pictures to do it: the children will 'read' them with you.
- Check the children are familiar with what the compound word picture cards show.
- Ask all of the children to close their eyes while you make a word on the caterpillar (such as 'postbox').
- Ask them all to open their eyes and 'read' the word together, pointing to each picture as they say it.
- Give each child a turn individually, making a new word each time.

Step down
- Read each word with the children.
- If a particular child is finding the task challenging, give them the opportunity to 'read' a word that has already been modelled by another child.

Step up
- Once a child has successfully 'read' a word, ask them to close their eyes while you change just one picture (for example, changing 'postbox' to 'postman') and ask them to read the new word accurately.

RHYME IT: WIN THE PICTURE BACK

What you need:
- Rhyming rule card (Resource 3)
- Rhyming pictures (Resource 4)

- Remind the children of the 'Win the picture' game.
- Explain that you are going to play the game again, but this time it is going to be a bit trickier.
- Explain that you have lots of pictures and you are going to see if the children can win them from you by guessing what they are. You are not going to say the name of the thing in the picture, but you are going to give them two clues. They have to listen to your clues and see whether they can guess what your picture is.
- Choose one of the rhyming pictures, but don't let the children see what it is. Read out the two clues for that picture and see who can guess what your picture is, e.g. 'I've got something that you can drive and it rhymes with "star".'
- If a child guesses correctly, give them the picture.
- When everyone has won at least one picture, explain that you are going to try to win them back — but this time you will give only one clue: the rhyming clue. Ask, for example: 'Who has the picture that rhymed with "star"?' (car) or 'Who had the picture that rhymed with "moon"?' (spoon).

Step down
- When you are winning the pictures back, choose only two children to listen for the rhyme each time.

Step up
- Giving a different rhyming clue when you try to win the picture back, e.g. for 'car', you could say, 'Who has the picture that rhymes with "bar"?'

WEEK 5

LISTEN FOR IT: LISTENING FOR COMPOUND WORDS ACTIVITY TWO

What you need:
- Sequencing caterpillar (Resource 5)
- Compound word picture cards (Resource 10): set two and word list

- Remind the children of the 'listening for compound words' game (from week 4). Explain that they will be playing the game again, using new pictures.
- Check the children are familiar with what the compound word pictures show. Take the first turn to make a compound word on the caterpillar, and read this together with the children. For example: 'Lady, bird: ladybird.'
- Say a new compound word (such as 'sunflower'), and ask a child to find the two pictures they need and sequence them on the caterpillar.
- When they have the right pictures in the right order, ask the children to 'read' the word together.

Step down
- If a child finds only the first picture, say the word again and leave a gap between the two words: for example, 'sun... flower'.
- If a child chooses the right pictures but puts them in the wrong order (e.g. 'flowersun'), 'read' the word together so they can hear that it does not sound right. Then ask the child to change the sequence to make the correct word.

Step up
- Challenge the children to change one picture to make a new word, e.g. they could change 'sunflower' to 'sunbed'.

CLAP IT: LISTENING FOR ONE OR TWO SYLLABLES: FOOD

What you need:
- Syllable clap cards (Resource 1): one and two clap words
- Syllable pictures (Resource 7): food with one or two syllables

- Explain that you have lots of pictures: some of them show things with just one clap in their name and some show things with two. The children are going to help you sort them out by matching each to the right syllable clap card.
- Put the pictures face down on the table and ask children to take it in turns to choose one and name it.
- Ask everyone to get their hands ready to clap, and remember to say 'ready, steady, go' so that everyone claps at the same time. Then clap the word together, e.g. 'bis – cuit'.
- Say the word again and count on your fingers as you say each syllable so the children can see as well as hear how many syllables are in the word.
- Ask the children to match the word to the right syllable clap card, and check by saying the word as you touch each clap on the card.

Step down
- Say and clap the word represented by the picture first, so the children can copy your model.

Step up
- Instead of working as a group, give children turns individually to clap out each word.

SAY IT:
'READING' COMPOUND WORDS
ACTIVITY TWO

What you need:
- Sequencing caterpillar (Resource 5): two segments
- Compound word picture cards (Resource 10): set two and word list

- Remind the children of the 'reading compound words' game they played (from week 4). Explain that they will be playing the game again, using new pictures.
- Explain that you are going to make some words on the sequencing caterpillar, but again you are going to use pictures to do it: the children will 'read' them with you.
- Ask all of the children to close their eyes while you make a word on the caterpillar (such as 'starfish').
- Ask them all to open their eyes and 'read' the word together, pointing to each picture as they say it.
- Give each child a turn individually, making a new word each time.

Step down
- Read each word with the children.
- If a particular child is finding the task challenging, give them the opportunity to 'read' a word that has already been modelled by another child.

Step up
- Once a child has successfully 'read' a word, ask them to close their eyes while you change just one picture (e.g. changing 'sunflower' to 'sunbed') and ask them to read the new word accurately.

RHYME IT:
'I SPY' RHYMING: TWO OPTIONS

What you need:
- Rhyming rule card (Resource 3)
- Rhyming pictures (Resource 4)

- Explain that you are going to play 'I Spy', but you are not going to say what letter each word starts with. Instead, you are going to say what it rhymes with.
- Using the rhyming rule card, remind the children again of the rhyming rule: the first sound is different but the rest is the same.
- Put out two pictures (such as a train and a key) and give the children an 'I Spy' rhyming clue, e.g. 'I spy a picture-word that rhymes with "plane".'
- Work through the first clue together as a group, finding the picture representing a word that rhymes.
- Give each child their own turn, choosing two new pictures each time.

Step down
- Say the clue while showing each picture, so the children can hear the possible rhymes and non-rhymes, e.g. 'plane' and 'train' or 'plane' and 'key'.

Step up
- Give the children three options to choose from.

WEEK 6

LISTEN FOR IT: COMPOUND WORD CHAINS

What you need:
- Sequencing caterpillar (Resource 5): two segments
- Compound word picture cards (Resource 10): set one and word chain

- Explain that you are going to make eight different words on the sequencing caterpillar using just pictures. Everyone will have a turn, and will need to change just one picture each time to make a new word. They will have to listen really carefully to the word, so they know which pictures they need.
- Assemble the starting word on the caterpillar and read it together, e.g. 'dragonfly'.
- Pass the caterpillar to the first child and say the new word, e.g. 'firefly'.
- Ask the child to decide which picture they need to change, and to find the new picture to put in its place.
- Read the new word together and pass on the caterpillar to the next child, repeating this until all of the words have been made and read.

Step down
○ Give the children just two options to choose from to make the new word.

Step up
○ Repeat the activity, choosing a different child to start the chain so everyone makes a different word.

CLAP IT: LISTENING FOR ONE OR TWO SYLLABLES: ANIMALS

What you need:
- Syllable clap cards (Resource 1): one and two clap words
- Syllable picture cards (Resource 7): animals with one or two syllables

- Explain that you have lots of pictures: some of them show things with just one clap in their name and some show things with two. The children are going to help you sort them out by matching each to the right syllable clap card.
- Put the pictures face down on the table and ask children to take it in turns to choose one and name it.
- Ask everyone to get their hands ready to clap, and remember to say 'ready, steady, go' so that everyone claps at the same time. Then clap the word together, e.g. 'ti – ger'.
- Say the word again and count on your fingers as you say each syllable so the children can see as well as hear how many syllables are in the word.
- Ask the children to match the word to the right syllable clap card, and check it by saying the word as you touch each clap on the card.

Step down
○ Say and clap the word represented by the picture first, so the children can copy your model.

Step up
○ Instead of working as a group, give children turns individually to clap out the word.

SAY IT: BLENDING SYLLABLES

What you need:
- Syllable-blending picture cards (Resource 11)

- Ensure the children are familiar with what the syllable-blending picture cards show.
- Explain that you are going to choose a picture, but you are not going to let the children see which one it is. You will say its word very slowly, one syllable at a time. The children have to listen very carefully and see if they can put the syllables together to say the word.
- Choose a card, and then hide the picture from the children.
- Say the syllables of the word slowly, e.g. if you choose the 'monkey' card, say, 'mon… key'.
- Ask the children to recognise and say the word.
- When they have said the word accurately, show them the picture.
- Give each child a turn to complete the activity independently.

Step down
○ Leave a shorter gap between the syllables.

Step up
○ Leave a longer gap between the syllables.
○ Use three syllable words (examples in Resource 7).

RHYME IT: 'I SPY' RHYMING: THREE OPTIONS

What you need:
- Rhyming rule card (Resource 3)
- Rhyming pictures (Resource 4)

- Remind the children of the 'I Spy' game they played (from week 5).
- Explain that you are going to play the game again, but this time they will have three pictures to choose from.
- Using the rhyming rule card, remind the children again of the rhyming rule: the first sound is different but the rest is the same.
- Put out 3 pictures (such as a train, a key and a spoon) and give the children an 'I spy' rhyming clue, e.g. 'I spy a picture-word that rhymes with "plane".'
- Work through the first clue together as a group, finding the one that rhymes. Give each child their own turn, choosing three new pictures each time.

Step down
○ Say the clue while showing each picture, so the children can hear whether the words rhyme, such as 'plane' and 'train', 'plane' and 'key' or 'plane' and 'spoon'.

Step up
○ Give the children four or more options to choose from.

WEEK 7

LISTEN FOR IT: COMPOUND WORD CHAIN RACE

What you need:
- Sequencing caterpillar (Resource 5): two segments
- Compound word picture cards (Resource 10): set two and word chain

- Remind the children of the compound word chain activity they did in the previous session (from week 6).
- Explain that you are going to make eight different words on the sequencing caterpillar using pictures again, but this time you are going to work together to see how quickly you can make all of the words. Everyone will have a turn, and will just need to change one picture each time to make the new word. The children will have to listen carefully so they know which pictures they need to use.
- Assemble the starting word on the caterpillar and read it together, e.g. 'sunflower'.
- Start a timer.
- Pass the caterpillar to the first child and say the new word, e.g. 'sunbed'.
- Ask the child to decide which picture they need to change, and to find the new picture to put in its place.
- Read the new word together and pass on the caterpillar to the next child and say the next word. Repeat this until all of the words have been made and read. Then stop the clock.

Step down
- Give the children just two options to choose from to make the new word.

Step up
- Repeat the activity, trying to beat your previous time.

CLAP IT: LISTENING FOR ONE, TWO AND THREE SYLLABLES: TRANSPORT

What you need:
- Syllable clap cards (Resource 1): one, two and three clap words
- Syllable picture cards (Resource 7): transport with one, two or three syllables

- Explain that you have lots of picture: some of them show things with just one clap in their name, some show things with two and some show things with three. The children are going to help you sort them out by matching each to the right syllable clap card.
- Put the pictures face down on the table and ask children to take it in turns to choose one and name it.
- Ask everyone to get their hands ready to clap, and remember to say 'ready, steady, go' so that everyone claps at the same time. Then clap the word together, e.g. 'trac – tor'.
- Say the word again and count on your fingers as you say each syllable so the children can see as well as hear how many syllables are in the word.
- Ask the children to match the word to the right syllable clap card, and check it by saying the word as you touch each clap on the card.

Step down
- Say and clap the word represented by the picture first, so the children can copy your model.

Step up
- Instead of working as a group, give children turns individually to clap out the word.

SAY IT: SYLLABLE-BLENDING CHOICE

What you need:
- Syllable-blending picture cards (Resource 11)

- Explain that you have some pairs of words that sound nearly the same. You are going to choose one of them and say it very slowly, one clap at a time. The children have to listen carefully and see if they can put the syllables together to say the word.
- Put a picture pair face up on the table.
- Say one of the words, leaving a long gap between the syllables, e.g. put out 'camel' and 'carrot', and say, 'ca… mel'.
- Ask the children to recognise and say the word. Give each child a turn to complete the activity independently, choosing a different pair of pictures each time.

Step down
- Put a shorter gap between syllables so it is easier for the children to blend the word back together.

Step up
- Hide the pictures so the children can guess the word only by blending it back together.

RHYME IT: YES/NO RHYMING ACTIVITY ONE

What you need:
- Yes/no cards (Resource 12): two sets
- Rhyming pictures (Resource 4)

- Use a clear setting for this activity, which involves the children running between two points. If you would prefer to keep the activity table based, give each child a counter to put on a 'yes' or 'no' card.
- Space out one set of 'yes' and 'no' cards at either side of a clear, open area, and keep one set for yourself.
- Explain that you have lots of pictures: some of them are words that rhyme, but some don't. You are going to say two words, and the children have to listen carefully to decide whether they rhyme. If the words rhyme, the children should run to the 'yes' card; if they don't, the children should run to the 'no' card. The children should take it in turns to complete this activity.
- Choose two of the rhyming picture cards, show them to the children and name them.
- Count down 'three, two, one, go' to signal for the children to run to the correct card. The children take it in turns to run.
- Once the children have run to a card, say the words again and show either the 'yes' or 'no' card to reveal whether the children were right.

Step down
- Play the game as a group activity so children always have a model to copy.

Step up
- Hide the pictures so the children can only listen to you saying the words.

WEEK 8

LISTEN FOR IT: STAND-UP SIT-DOWN: LETTER SOUNDS

What you need:
- Letter cards

- Explain that you are going to say two letter sounds but you are not going to show the letters to the children. You will start making one of the sounds and the children have to listen carefully for when the sound changes. As soon as they hear the sound change, they must stand up and stay standing up until they hear it change back again. When they hear it change again, they can sit back down.
- Choose two letter sounds and start making a sequence. For example: 'p…p…p…p…p… i…i…i…i…i…i…p…p…p…p'.
- You could continue playing this game as a group, or give each child a turn by themselves.

Step down
- Choose very different letter sounds, such as /s/ and /a/.

Step up
- Choose very similar letter sounds, such as /a/ and /i/ or /p/ and /t/.
- Put the letter sounds in very short words, such as 'in' and 'it'.

CLAP IT: LISTENING FOR ONE, TWO AND THREE SYLLABLES: MINIBEASTS

What you need:
- Syllable clap cards (Resource 1): one, two and three clap words
- Syllable picture cards (Resource 7): minibeasts with one, two or three syllables

- Explain that you have lots of pictures: some of them show things with just one clap in their name, some show things with two and some show things with three. The children are going to help you sort them out by matching each to the right syllable clap card.
- Put the pictures face down on the table and ask children to take it in turns to choose one and name it.
- Ask everyone to get their hands ready to clap, and remember to say 'ready, steady, go' so that everyone claps at the same time. Then clap the word together, e.g. 'la – dy – bird'.
- Say the word again and count on your fingers as you say each syllable so the children can see as well as hear how many syllables were in the word.
- Ask the children to match the word to the right syllable clap card, and check it by saying the word as you touch each clap on the card.

Step down
- Say and clap the word represented by the picture first, so the children can copy your model.

Step up
- Instead of working as a group, give children turns individually to clap out the word.

SAY IT:
VOWEL-CONSONANT (VC) WORD-MAKING
ACTIVITY ONE

What you need:
- Sequencing caterpillar (Resource 5) two segments
- Letters 'a', 'i', 't', 's', 'f', 'n' and 'm'

- Explain that you are going to make some short words on the sequencing caterpillar. The children will need two letters to make each word. They should take it in turns to complete this activity.
- Present the children with the letters 'a', 'i', 't', 's', 'f', 'n' and 'm'.
- Check that the children know the letters by asking them to point to the correct one as you say each sound.
- Show the children how the activity will work by making a word on the caterpillar and reading it together. Words you can make with these letters are 'it', 'in', 'is', 'if', 'am', 'at', 'as' and 'an'.
- Change a letter to make a new word. For example, change 'it' to 'in' and read the word together again.

Step down
○ Continue reading the words as a group.

Step up
○ Change both letters to make a completely new word.

RHYME IT:
RHYME MATCH
ACTIVITY ONE

What you need:
- Rhyming rule card (Resource 3)
- Rhyming pictures (Resource 4): one and two syllable words

- Using the rhyming rule card, explain the rule about rhyming words: the first sound is different and the rest of the word sounds the same.
- Give each child two pictures that don't rhyme. Make sure that one of the pair is a two syllable word and the other has only one syllable (e.g. 'coat' and 'flower'), to make it easier for the children to hear the rhyme.
- Tell the children that you have a picture that rhymes with one of them, and they have to listen carefully to find out which one it is.
- Say each word so the children can hear the possible rhyme, e.g. 'boat, coat, or boat, flower?'
- Make sure you vary whether the target rhyme is said first or second.

Step down
○ Talk about the last sound in the target word and be explicit about listening for that sound.

Step up
○ Ask children to name each picture (instead of doing it yourself), challenging them to hear the rhyme themselves.

WEEK 9

 ## LISTEN FOR IT: STAND-UP SIT-DOWN: WORDS

What you need:
- VC word lists (Resource 13)

- Explain that you are going to play the 'stand-up sit-down' game again (from week 8), but this time it will be trickier.
- You are going to say two different short words for the children. As soon as they hear the word change, they must stand up and stay standing up until they hear it change back again. When they hear it change again, they can sit back down.
- Choose two words from the VC word list, and start making a sequence. For example: 'it…it….it…in…in…in…is…is'.
- You could continue playing this game as a group, or give each child a turn by themselves.

Step down
- Choose the 'step down' words from the list: words in which both sounds change, to make the change easier for children to hear.

Step up
- Choose the 'step up' words from the list: words in which the sounds are very similar, so the change is harder to hear.

 ## CLAP IT: LISTENING FOR ONE, TWO, THREE AND FOUR SYLLABLES: FOOD

What you need:
- Syllable clap cards (Resource 1): one, two, three and four clap words
- Syllable picture cards (Resource 7): food with one, two, three and four syllables

- Explain that you have lots of pictures: this time, they may show things with one, two, three or four claps in their name. The children are going to help you sort them out by matching each to the right syllable clap card.
- Put the pictures face down on the table and ask the children to take it in turns to choose one and name it.
- Ask everyone to get their hands ready to clap, and remember to say 'ready, steady, go' so that everyone claps at the same time. Then clap the word together, e.g. 'wa – ter – me – lon'.
- Say the word again and count on your fingers as you say each syllable so the children can see as well as hear how many syllables are in the word.
- Ask the children to match the word to the right syllable clap card, and check it by saying the word as you touch each clap on the card.

Step down
- Say and clap the word represented by the picture first, so the children can copy your model.

Step up
- Instead of working as a group, give children turns individually to clap out the word.

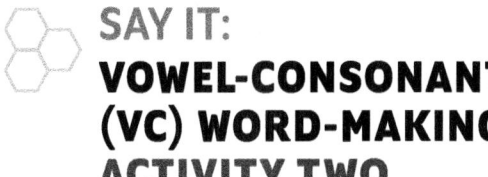

SAY IT:
VOWEL-CONSONANT (VC) WORD-MAKING
ACTIVITY TWO

What you need:
- Sequencing caterpillar (Resource 5): two segments
- Letters: 'a', 'i', 't', 's', 'f', 'n', 'm', 'p', 'u' and 'o'

- Explain that you are going to make some short words on the sequencing caterpillar again (from week 8). The children will need two letters to make each word. They should take it in turns to complete this activity.
- Present the children with the letters 'a', 'i', 't', 's', 'f', 'n', 'm', 'p', 'u' and 'o'.
- Check that the children know the letters by asking them to point to the correct one as you say each sound.
- Show the children how the activity will work by making a word on the caterpillar and reading it together. Words you can make with these letters are 'it', 'in', 'is', 'if', 'am', 'at', 'as', 'an', 'on', 'of', 'us' and 'up'.
- Change a letter to make a new word, e.g. change 'on' to 'an' and read it together again.
- Give each child a turn.

Step down
○ Continue reading the words as a group.

Step up
○ Change both letters to make a completely new word.

RHYME IT:
RHYME MATCH
ACTIVITY TWO

What you need:
- Rhyming rule card (Resource 3)
- Rhyming pictures (Resource 4): one syllable words

- Using the rhyming rule card, explain the rule about rhyming words: the first sound is different and the rest of the word sounds the same.
- Give each child two pictures that don't rhyme. This time, make sure both words in the pair have only one syllable.
- Tell the children that you have a picture that rhymes with one of them, and they have to listen carefully to find out which one it is.
- Say each word so the children can hear the possible rhyme: for example, 'car, star, or sock, star?'
- Make sure you vary whether the target rhyme is said first or second.

Step down
○ Talk about the last sound in the target word and be explicit about listening for that sound.

Step up
○ Ask children to name each picture (instead of doing it yourself), challenging them to hear the rhyme themselves.

WEEK 10

LISTEN FOR IT: SOUND RUN-AROUND

What you need:
- Four cards or posters, each showing a letter that the children are encountering in phonics lessons

- Use a clear setting for this activity, which involves the children moving between four points. If you would prefer to keep the activity table based, give each child a counter to put by a letter.
- Put four letters up on different walls in a room, or spread them out in a clear, open area.
- Show the children where they are, saying each letter's sound as you do so.
- Ask the children to wait in the middle of the space until you say one of the sounds, and then to move to the letter representing the sound they hear.
- When all of the children have moved to the letter you have sounded, say the sound together.
- Start by having all of the children moving together. When they are confident with the activity, give each child their own turn so they are not reliant on copying others.

Step down
- Reduce the choice of letters to two.
- Choose letters that make 'long' sounds (sounds that can be made continuously), such as s /m /f /n sounds.

Step up
- Choose one child to be the 'teacher' and say the sounds for the other children.
- Choose letters that make 'short' sounds (sounds that cannot be made continuously), such as p /t /ck /b sounds.

CLAP IT: LISTENING FOR ONE, TWO, THREE AND FOUR SYLLABLES: ANIMALS

What you need:
- Syllable clap cards (Resource 1): one, two, three and four clap words
- Syllable picture cards (Resource 7): animals with one, two, three or four syllables

- Explain that you have lots of pictures: they may show things with one, two, three or four claps (syllables) in their name. The children are going to help you sort them out by matching each to the right syllable clap card.
- Put the pictures face down on the table and ask the children to take it in turns to choose one and name it.
- Ask everyone to get their hands ready to clap, and remember to say 'three, two, one, go' so that everyone claps at the same time. Then clap the word together: for example, 'rhi – no – cer – os'.
- Say the word again and count on your fingers as you say each syllable so the children can see as well as hear how many syllables are in the word.
- Ask the children to match the word to the right syllable clap card, and check it by saying the word as you touch each clap on the card.

Step down
- Say and clap the word represented by the picture first, so the children can copy your model.

Step up
- Instead of working as a group, give children turns individually to clap out the word.

SAY IT: CONSONANT-VOWEL (CV) BLENDING: LONG SOUNDS

What you need:
- Letters: 'long' consonant letters that the children are encountering in phonics lessons (e.g. m /n /f /s /v /z /sh)
- Vowel cards (Resource 8)
- Sequencing caterpillar (Resource 5): two segments

- Explain that you are going to make some short words on the sequencing caterpillar. The children will need two sounds to make each word. Some of the words will be real words and some might be nonsense words.
- Explain that you are going stroke the caterpillar while you say the sounds to make the word. You always need to stroke the caterpillar the same way, starting at his head, and you can't stop while you are saying the sounds.
- Make a word on the sequencing caterpillar: use a consonant letter on the caterpillar's head and a vowel card next (e.g. 's' and 'ee').
- Stroke the caterpillar as you say the sounds together, modelling how to keep the sounds going so they blend into each other, e.g. 'see'.
- Make a new word and let each child have a turn at reading it.

Step down
- Continue reading the words as a group.
- Keep the first sound the same and change only the vowel.

Step up
- Change both sounds each time.

RHYME IT: YES/NO RHYMING ACTIVITY TWO

What you need:
- Yes/no cards (Resource 12): two sets
- Rhyming pictures (Resource 4)
- Rhyme judgement pictures (Resource 17)

- Use a clear setting for this activity, which involves the children running between two points. If you would prefer to keep the activity table based, give each child a counter to put on a yes or no card.
- Space out one set of yes/no cards at either side of a clear, open area, and keep one set for yourself.
- Remind the children of the 'yes/no rhyming' game they played (from week 7), but this time the words sound nearly the same.
- Explain that you have lots of pictures: some of them have words that rhyme, but some don't. You are going to say two words, and the children have to listen carefully to decide whether they rhyme. If the words rhyme, the children should run to the 'yes' card; if they don't, the children should run to the 'no' card. The children should take it in turns to complete this activity.
- Choose two of the rhyming picture cards, show them to the children and name them.
- Count down 'three, two, one, go' to signal for the children to run to the correct card.
- Once the children have run to a card, say the words again and show either the 'yes' or 'no' card to reveal whether the children were right.

Step down
- Play the game as a group activity so children always have a model to copy.

Step up
- Hide the pictures so the children can only listen to you saying the words.

WEEK 11

LISTEN FOR IT: WORD RUN AROUND

What you need:
- Two pairs of pictures to stick on the walls from the minimal pair pictures (Resource 15)
- It would be helpful to have an extra matching set for the adult to hold.

- If you would prefer to keep the activity table based, give each child a counter to put by a picture.
- Put four pictures up on different walls in the room, e.g. 'tea', 'key', 'four' and 'door'.
- Show the children where they are, naming each picture as you do.
- The children wait in the middle of the room until you name one of the pictures. They then have to move to the picture that they heard. When all of the children have moved to the picture, turn your picture around and say it again so that they can check whether they have the right one.
- Start the activity having all of the children moving together. When they feel confident, try giving each child their own turn so they are not reliant on copying others.

Step down
- Reduce the choice of pictures to one pair.

Step up
- One child can be the 'teacher' and name the pictures for the other children.

CLAP IT: SAYING WORDS WITH ONE, TWO AND THREE SYLLABLE CLAPS: TRANSPORT

What you need:
- Syllable clap cards for one, two and three clap words (Resource 1)
- Transport pictures with one, two and three syllables (Resource 7)

- Explain that you have lots of pictures: this time, they may show things with one, two or three claps (syllables) in their name, e.g. bike (one clap), ice-cream van (three claps). The children are going to help you sort them out by matching them to the right syllable clap card, but this time it will be trickier because they are going to say the words themselves.
- Put the pictures face down on the table and ask the children to take it in turns to choose one.
- Ask the child to say the word and clap it out themselves. See whether they can match it to the right syllable clap card, and check it themselves by saying the word as they touch each clap on the card.

Step down
- If any children are finding this challenging, ask the other members of the group to help by all clapping the word together.

Step up
- See if the children can decide the number of syllables by saying the word but not clapping it.

SAY IT:
CONSONANT-VOWEL (CV) BLENDING: SHORT SOUNDS

What you need:
- Letters: 'short' consonant letters that the children are encountering in phonics lessons (e.g. t /p /ck /b /d /g)
- Vowel cards (Resource 8)
- Sequencing caterpillar (Resource 5): two segments

- CV blending: short sounds
- Explain that you are going to make some short words on the sequencing caterpillar. The children will need two sounds to make each word. Some of the words will be real words and some might be nonsense words.
- Explain that you are going stroke the caterpillar while you say the sounds to make the word. You always need to stroke the caterpillar the same way, starting at his head, and you can't stop while you are saying the sounds.
- Make a word on the sequencing caterpillar: use a consonant letter on the caterpillar's head and a vowel card next, e.g. 'b' and 'ow'.
- Stroke the caterpillar as you say the sounds together, modelling how to keep the sounds going so they blend into each other, e.g. 'bow'.
- Make a new word and let each child have a turn at reading it.

Step down
- Continue reading the words as a group.
- Keep the initial sound the same and only change the vowel.

Step up
- Change both sounds each time.

RHYME IT:
RHYMING: ODD ONE OUT ACTIVITY ONE

What you need:
- Rhyming rule card (Resource 3)
- Rhyme judgement pictures (Resource 17)

- Remind them of the rule about rhyming words; the first sound is different and the rest of the word sounds the same.
- Put out three pictures (two rhyming words and one non-rhyming word). Explain to the children that two of the words will rhyme and one of them will not. The children will complete this activity individually rather than at the same time.
- Say each word slowly for the children. See if they can spot the odd one out.
- Give each child a turn, changing the words each time.
- Make sure that the non-rhyming word is in a different place in the sequence each time.

Step down
- Discuss the last sound in each word with the children, being explicit about listening for that sound.

Step up
- Ask the children to name each picture (instead of the adult) to see if they can then hear the rhyme themselves.

WEEK 12

LISTEN FOR IT: SPOT THE ERROR: INITIAL SOUNDS

What you need:
- A range of initial sound pictures (Resource 14)

- Explain that you are going to put three pictures out and name them, but you will say one word the wrong way.
- The children have to listen carefully and say 'stop!' as soon as they hear you make a mistake.
- Pick three pictures that start with the same sound and say the words for the children, but on one word use the wrong first sound. e.g. 'table, kent, two' instead of 'table, tent, two'.
- See if the children can listen for the word being said incorrectly.

Step down
- Repeat the sequence, emphasising the initial sounds.
- Take one picture away so they only have to listen to two and decide which was wrong.

Step up
- See if the children can name the word correctly.

CLAP IT: SAYING WORDS WITH ONE, TWO, THREE AND FOUR SYLLABLE CLAPS: MINIBEASTS

What you need:
- Syllable clap cards for one, two, three and four clap words (Resource 1)
- Minibeast pictures with one, two three and four syllables (Resource 7)

- Explain that you have lots of pictures: this time, they may show things with one, two, three or four claps in their name. They are going to help you sort them out by matching them to the right syllable clap card, but this time it will be trickier because they are going to say the words themselves.
- Put the pictures face down on the table and ask the children to take it in turns to choose one.
- Ask the child to say the word and clap it out themselves. See whether they can match it to the right syllable clap card, and check it themselves by saying the word as they touch each clap on the card.

Step down
- If the child is finding this challenging, ask the other children to help by all clapping the word together.

Step up
- See if the child can decide the number of syllables by saying the word without clapping it.

SAY IT: WORD TAKEAWAY

What you need:
- Word takeaway lists (Resource 16): compound words

- Explain to the children that that you are going to say a word, and then ask them to take part of the word away to make a new word. The children will complete this activity individually rather than at the same time.
- Complete the first word together, e.g. 'What is skateboard with no board?'
- Give each child a turn with a different word, and see if they can take part of the word away by themselves.

Step down
- Repeat the compound word and leave a small gap between the words, e.g. 'skate...board'.

Step up
- Ask them to take first part of the word away, e.g. 'what is skateboard with no skate?'

RHYME IT: RHYMING: ODD ONE OUT ACTIVITY TWO

What you need:
- Rhyming rule card (Resource 3)
- Rhyme judgement pictures (Resource 17)

- Explain that you are going to play odd one out again (from week 11), but this week the words sound more similar.
- Put out three pictures (two rhyming words and one non-rhyming word). Explain to the children that two of the words will rhyme and one of them will not. The children will complete this activity individually rather than at the same time.
- Say each word slowly for the children. See if they can spot the odd one out.
- Give each child a turn, changing the words each time.
- Make sure that the non-rhyming word is in a different place in the sequence each time.

Step down
- Discuss the last sound in each word with the children, being explicit about listening for that sound.

Step up
- Ask the children to name each picture (instead of the adult) to see if they can then hear the rhyme themselves.

WEEK 13

LISTEN FOR IT: SPOT THE ERROR: FINAL SOUNDS

What you need:
- Final sound pictures (Resource 18)

- Explain that you are going to put three pictures out and name them, but you will say one the wrong way.
- The children have to listen carefully and say 'stop!' as soon as they hear you make a mistake.
- Pick three pictures that end with the same sound and say the words for the children, but on one word use the wrong final sound, e.g. if you choose 't' at the ends of words you might say 'hat, cat, sweek' instead of 'hat, cat, sweet'.
- See if the children can listen for the word being said incorrectly.

Step down
- Repeat the sequence, emphasising the final sound.
- Take one picture away, so that the children only have to listen to two words and decide which one was wrong.

Step up
- See if the children can name the word correctly.

CLAP IT: SYLLABLE RUN AROUND: FOOD

What you need:
- Syllable clap cards for one, two and three clap words (Resource 1)
- Food pictures with one, two and three syllables (Resource 7)

- Put one, two and three syllable clap cards up on different walls in the room. If you would prefer to keep the activity table based, give each child a counter to put by a syllable clap card.
- Show the children where the syllable clap cards are, clapping each word as you do.
- The children wait in the middle of the room until you show them a picture.
- Start by clapping the word out together, then say 'ready, steady, go'. The children run to the right number of claps (syllables) for the picture. Once the children have chosen a clap card, clap the syllables together to check if they are right.
- If the children are confident, you can try just showing the children the picture and seeing if they can say the word out loud without guidance. Then say 'ready, steady, go!' and see if the children can work out the right number of syllables themselves.

Step down
- Keep clapping the words out together.

Step up
- Children have individual turns.
- One child can be the 'teacher', naming the pictures for the other children.

SAY IT: VOWEL-CONSONANT (VC) WORD CHAINS

What you need:
- Sequencing caterpillar (Resource 5): two segments
- Word chain list (Resource 19) and corresponding letter cards

- Explain that you are all going to work together to see how many short words you can make on the sequencing caterpillar. The children will need to change one letter each time to make a new word.
- Choose a word chain, e.g. 'is; in; on; of' etc., and put out the letters you will need from the resource. Check that the children know the letters by asking them to point as you say each sound.
- Make the starting word on the caterpillar and read it together.
- Pass the caterpillar to the first child and say the second word in the word chain. See if they can change one of the letters to make the new word, and if they are able to read it.
- Continue to pass the caterpillar round the group, making a new word in the chain each time.

Step down
- Continue to work together as a group to complete the word chain.

Step up
- Play the game as a timed activity and see how many words the children can make in a minute.
- Play it again and see whether the children can beat their previous score.

RHYME IT: WIN THE RHYME ACTIVITY ONE

What you need:
- Rhyming pictures (Resource 4)
- Win the rhyme word lists (Resource 20)
- Letter cards corresponding to word list

- Explain that you are going to use some letters to make new rhymes. The children will complete this activity individually rather than at the same time.
- Choose a rhyming picture and show the group, e.g. 'car'. Choose a letter and explain that changing the word's first letter will make a new rhyming word, e.g. using the letter 'b' changes 'car' to 'bar'.
- Show the children a new rhyming picture and give them a letter.
- They need to change the first sound with their letter to make a new rhyming word and win the picture.
- Take it in turns until everyone has won a picture.

Step down
- Continue to work as a group.

Step up
- Do not name the picture or letter for the children.

39

WEEK 14

 ## LISTEN FOR IT: SAME OR DIFFERENT JUDGEMENT: FIRST SOUND – REAL WORDS

What you need:
- Same/different cue card (Resource 21)
- Same/different judgement word list – first sound, real words (Resource 22)
- Counters or similar

- Explain that you are going to say two words. They might be exactly the same or the first sound might be different, e.g. 'map' and 'map' or 'net' and 'pet'. The children will complete this activity individually rather than at the same time.
- The children have to listen carefully and if they think the words are the same, then they put their counter on the 'same' cue card. If the children think the words are different, then they put their counter on the 'different' cue card.
- Try the first one together so that the whole group can decide. Then let each child have an individual turn.

Step down
○ Give the children lots of chances to hear the pair of words.

Step up
○ Only give the children one chance to hear the pair of words.
○ Don't tell the children where in the word the sound might be different, e.g. beginning/middle/end.

 ## CLAP IT: SYLLABLE RUN AROUND: ANIMALS

What you need:
- Syllable clap cards for one, two, three and four clap words (Resource 1)
- Animal pictures with one, two, three and four syllables (Resource 7)

- Put one, two, three and four syllable clap cards up on different walls in the room. If you would prefer to keep the activity table based, give each child a counter to put by a syllable clap card.
- Show the children where they are, clapping each picture as you do.
- The children wait in the middle of the room until you show them an animal picture.
- Start by clapping the word out together, then say 'ready, steady, go'. The children run to the right number of claps for the word. Once the children have chosen a clap card, clap the syllables together to check if they are right.
- If the children are confident, you can try just showing the children the picture and seeing if they can say the word out loud without guidance. Then say 'ready, steady, go!' and see if the children can work out the right number of syllables themselves.

Step down
○ Keep clapping the words out together.

Step up
○ Children have individual turns.
○ One child can be the 'teacher', naming the words for the other children.

SAY IT:
CONSONANT-VOWEL-CONSONANT (CVC) WORD CHAINS ACTIVITY ONE

What you need:
- Sequencing caterpillar (Resource 5): three segments
- Word chain list (Resource 19) and corresponding letter cards

- Explain that you are all going to work together to make words on the sequencing caterpillar, but this time it will be trickier because they will have three sounds in them rather than two (from week 13).
- The children will need to change one letter each time to make a new word. It might be the first sound in the word or the last sound.
- Choose a CVC word chain, e.g. 'cat; mat; man; map' etc., and put out the letters you will need. Check that the children know the letters by asking them to point as you say each sound.
- Make the starting word on the caterpillar and read it together. Remind the children that the middle letter is going to stay the same.
- Pass the caterpillar to the first child and say the second word in the word chain. See if they can change one of the letters to make the new word, and if they are able to read it.
- Continue to pass the caterpillar round, making a new word in the chain each time.

Step down
- Continue to work together as a group to complete the word chain

Step up
- Play the game as a timed activity and see how many words the children can make in a minute.
- Play it again and see whether the children can beat their previous score.

RHYME IT:
PASS THE PARCEL: RHYME GENERATION

What you need:
- Rhyming rule card (Resource 3)
- Rhyming pictures (Resource 4)
- An object to pass around e.g. a ball
- Optional for step down – letters
- Optional for step up – timer

- Put out a picture of an easy rhyming word e.g. 'cat' or 'chair'.
- Explain to the children that they are going to think of as many rhyming words as they can. They can be real words or silly rhymes. They can only pass on the 'parcel' when they have said a rhyming word.
- See how many words the group can make from each starter word.

Step down
- Put out some letters to help children think of different sounds they can use to make a new rhyme.

Step up
- Use a timer to see how many words the group can make in a minute.

WEEK 15

LISTEN FOR IT: SAME OR DIFFERENT JUDGEMENT: FIRST SOUND – NONSENSE WORDS

What you need:
- Same/different cue card (Resource 21)
- Same/different judgement word list – first sound, nonsense words (Resource 22)
- Counters or similar

- Explain that you are going to say two nonsense words. They might be exactly the same or the first sound might be different, e.g. 'mal' and 'mal' or 'biv' and 'tiv'. The children will complete this activity individually rather than at the same time.
- The children have to listen carefully and if they think the words are the same, then they put their counter on the 'same' cue card. If the children think the words are different, then they put their counter on the 'different' cue card
- Try the first one together so that the whole group can decide. Then let each child have an individual turn.

Step down
- Give the children lots of chances to hear the pair of words.

Step up
- Only give the children one chance to hear the pair of words.
- Don't tell the children where in the word the sound might be different, e.g. beginning/middle/end.

CLAP IT: SYLLABLE TAKEAWAY

What you need:
- Word takeaway lists (Resource 16)

- Explain to the children that you are going to say a word and then ask them to take one clap (syllable) away to make a new word. The children will complete this activity individually rather than at the same time.
- Do the first one together, e.g. 'What is monkey with no mon?'
- Give each child a turn with a different word. Say a word for them and tell them which part they need to take away, e.g. 'what would 'carpet' be with no 'car'?'

Step down
- Repeat the word leaving a small gap between the syllables, e.g. 'mon...key'.

Step up
- Ask the children to take the second syllable of the word away e.g. 'what is monkey with no key?'

SAY IT: CONSONANT-VOWEL-CONSONANT (CVC) WORD CHAINS ACTIVITY TWO

What you need:
- Sequencing caterpillar (Resource 5): three segments
- Word chain list (Resource 19) and corresponding letter cards

- Explain that you are all going to work together to make words on the sequencing caterpillar, but this time they will have three sounds in them and any of the sounds might change. The children will still only need to change one letter each time to make a new word but it might be the first, middle or last sound in the word.
- Choose a CVC word chain, e.g. 'peg; beg; bag; bat' etc., and put out the letters you will need. Check that the children know the letters by asking them to point as you say each sound.
- Make the starting word on the caterpillar and read it together.
- Pass the caterpillar to the first child and say the second word in the word chain. See if they can change one of the letters to make the new word, and if they are able to read it.
- Continue to pass the caterpillar round, making a new word in the chain each time.

Step down
○ Continue to work together as a group to complete the word chain.

Step up
○ Play the game as a timed activity and see how many words the children can make in a minute.
○ Play it again and see whether the children can beat their previous score.

RHYME IT: RHYME AROUND THE CIRCLE

What you need:
- Rhyming rule card (Resource 3)
- Win the rhyme lists (Resource 20)
- Rhyming pictures (Resource 4)
- Letter cards

- Explain that the children are going to use some letters to see how many rhymes they can make for each word. The children will complete this activity individually rather than at the same time.
- Choose a rhyming picture to start the circle, e.g. 'sun', and show the group. Then give each child a letter from the list.
- Pass the picture around the circle. Each child must use their letter to make a new rhyming word.

Step down
○ Work as a group to make all of the new rhyming words.

Step up
○ Use a timer and see how long it takes to make all of the new rhyming words.

WEEK 16

LISTEN FOR IT: SAME OR DIFFERENT JUDGEMENT: LAST SOUND – REAL WORDS

What you need:
- Same/different cue card (Resource 21)
- Same/different judgement word list – final sound, real words (Resource 22)
- Counters or similar

- Explain that you are going to say two words. They might be exactly the same or the last sound might be different, e.g. 'sit' and 'sit' or 'log' and 'lot'. The children will complete this activity individually rather than at the same time.
- The children have to listen carefully and if they think the words are the same, they put their counter on the 'same' card. If they think the words are different, then they put their counter on the 'different' card.
- Try the first one together so that the whole group can decide. Then let each child have an individual turn.

Step down
○ Give the children lots of chances to hear the pair of words.

Step up
○ Only give the children one chance to hear the pair of words.
○ Don't tell the children where in the word the sound might be different, e.g. beginning/middle/end.

CLAP IT: SYLLABLE DICE

What you need:
- Syllable pictures (Resource 7)
- Game board (Resource 23) or a board game of your own choosing.
- A counter for each child

- Explain that the children are going to play a game but they are not going to use a dice. Instead you are going to pick up a picture and clap the syllables. However many claps it has, that is how many spaces the children can move.
- Put the syllable pictures in a pile face down. Each child takes it in turns to pick up a picture, clap the syllables and count how many spaces they can move their counter.
- Once they have moved, the next child has a turn. The winner is the first child to get to the end.

Step down
○ Clap the words all together.

Step up
○ Do not name the picture for the children and see whether they can clap out the word independently.
○ Encourage the children to think of a different word that gives them more claps and lets them move more spaces, e.g. 'bicycle' instead of 'bike'.

SAY IT:
SOUND TAKEAWAY

What you need:
- Word takeaway lists (Resource 16)

- Explain that you are going to say a word, and then you will ask the children to take one sound away to make a new word. The children will complete this activity individually rather than at the same time.
- Do the first one together, e.g. 'What is dice with no d?'
- Give each child a turn with a different word. Tell them to take a specific sound away, e.g. 'what is 'ditch' with no 'd'?'

Step down
- If a child is finding it challenging, demonstrate with a rhyming word, e.g. 'rice with no 'r' is ice... dice with no 'd' is...?'

Step up
- Give the children words that start with a consonant blend

RHYME IT:
RHYMING PAIRS

What you need:
- Rhyming pictures (Resource 4)

- Choose 6 pairs of rhyming pictures and put them face down on the table.
- Each child takes it in turns to turn over two pictures and see whether they rhyme or not.
- If they do rhyme, the child wins the pair. If not, they put them back in the same place and the next child takes a turn until all of the pictures have been won.

Step down
- Put the pictures face up.
- The adult names the pictures for the child.

Step up
- The child names the pictures independently.
- Use more pairs of pictures.

WEEK 17

 ## LISTEN FOR IT: SAME OR DIFFERENT JUDGEMENT: LAST SOUND – NONSENSE WORDS

What you need:
- Same/different cue card (Resource 21)
- Same/different judgement word list – last sound, nonsense words (Resource 22)
- Counters or similar

- Explain you are going to say two nonsense words. They might be exactly the same or the last sound might be different, e.g. 'cag' and 'cag' or 'pib' and 'pid'. The children will complete this activity individually rather than at the same time.
- The children have to listen carefully and if they think the words are the same, they put their counter on the 'same' card. If they think the words are different, then they put their counter on the 'different' card.
- Try the first one together so that the whole group can decide. Then let each child have an individual turn.

Step down
○ Give the children lots of chances to hear the pair of words.

Step up
○ Only give the children one chance to hear the pair of words.
○ Don't tell the children where in the word the sound might be different, e.g. beginning/middle/end.

 ## CLAP IT: STEPPING STONES: ONE, TWO AND THREE SYLLABLES

What you need:
- Syllable picture cards (Resource 7)
- Pieces of paper or PE equipment to make a path

- Use sheets of paper or similar to make a stepping stone path.
- Explain that the children need to go down the stepping stone path, but they will use pictures and clap out the syllables to decide how many steps they can move each.
- Choose a range of syllable pictures with one, two or three syllables in the words. Put the syllable pictures in a pile face down. Each child takes it in turns to pick up a picture, clap the syllables and count how many steps they can move.
- The first person to get to the end of the path is the winner.
- This activity may need to be modified for children with mobility issues. As an alternative, you can make a small version of the path on a table and the children can use counters.

Step down
○ Clap the words all together.

Step up
○ Do not name the picture for the child and see whether they can clap out the word independently.
○ Encourage the children to think of a different word that gives them more claps and lets them move more spaces e.g. 'bumble bee' instead of 'bee'.

SAY IT: SORT AND SAY: LONG AND SHORT SOUNDS

What you need:
- Initial sound pictures (Resource 14) that start with either 's' and 'd' or 'f' and 'b'
- Corresponding letter cards for the sounds you have chosen to use

- First, check that the children know the sound each letter makes and practise saying those sounds together a few times.
- Explain that you have got some pictures that start with those sounds, but they are all mixed up.
- The children help you sort out the pictures. You will name each picture and the children will decide which letter it needs to go on.
- Give each child a turn at listening to a word and putting it on a letter until all the pictures are sorted correctly.
- When you have the piles of pictures, take it in turns to say each picture with the right sound.

Step down
- Say the pictures together as a group.

Step up
- Mix together all four sets of pictures (s/d/f/b)

RHYME IT: RHYMING RUNAROUND ACTIVITY ONE

What you need:
- Rhyming rule card (Resource 3)
- Rhyming pictures (Resource 4)

- Remind the children of the rhyming rule 'the first sound is different but the rest is the same'.
- Explain that you have lots of pictures of words, some of them rhyme and some of them don't.
- You are going to show the group one picture at a time. The children have to name it and find a rhyming picture.
- Display the rhyming pictures around the room. Explain that the children will need to run to the picture that rhymes with the one you are holding.
- Choose a picture, show the children and ask them to name them. Countdown 'three, two, one, go' and the children need to run to the rhyming picture.
- Once the children have decided where to run, ask them to name their picture to see if they were correct.
- Give each child a turn.
- This activity may need to be modified for children with mobility issues, e.g. putting the pictures on a table.

Step down
- Play it as a group activity so children always have a model to copy.

Step up
- Choose two children to 'race' against each other. Show the picture to both children, then count down 'three, two, one, go' and see who is first to find the rhyming picture.

WEEK 18

 ## LISTEN FOR IT: SAME OR DIFFERENT JUDGEMENT: MIDDLE SOUND – REAL WORDS

What you need:
- Same/different cue card (Resource 21)
- Same/different judgement word list – middle sound, real words (Resource 22)
- Counters or similar

- Explain that you are going to say two words. They might be exactly the same or the middle sound might be different, e.g. 'bed' and 'bed' or 'sick' and 'sack'. The children will complete this activity individually rather than at the same time.
- The children have to listen carefully and if they think the words are the same, they put their counter on the 'same' card. If they think the words are different, then they put their counter on the 'different' card.
- Try the first one together so that the whole group can decide. Then let each child have an individual turn.

Step down
○ Use the step down long vowel word list (Resource 22)

Step up
○ Only give the children one chance to hear the pair of words.
○ Don't tell the children where in the word the sound might be different, e.g. beginning/ middle/end.

 ## CLAP IT: STEPPING STONES: ONE, TWO, THREE AND FOUR SYLLABLES

What you need:
- Syllable picture cards (Resource 7)
- Pieces of paper or PE equipment to make a path. (Remember that the path will need to be longer this week because clapping longer words means more steps!)

- Use sheets of paper or similar to make a stepping stone path.
- Explain that you are going to play the stepping stone game again (from week 17), but this week some pictures might have 4 claps in.
- Choose a range of syllable pictures with one, two, three or four syllables in the words. Put the syllable pictures in a pile face down. Each child takes it in turns to pick up a picture, clap the syllables and count how many steps they can move.
- The first person to get to the end of the path is the winner.
- This activity may need to be modified for children with mobility issues. As an alternative, you can make a small version of the path on a table and the children can use counters.

Step down
○ Clap the words all together as a group.

Step up
○ Do not name the picture for the child and see whether they clap out the syllables independently.
○ Encourage the children to think of a different word that gives them more claps and lets them move more spaces, e.g. 'chocolate cake' instead of 'cake'.

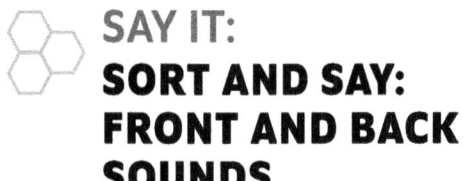

SAY IT:
SORT AND SAY: FRONT AND BACK SOUNDS

What you need:
- Initial sound pictures (Resource 14) that start with either 't' and 'ck' or 'd' and 'g'
- Corresponding letter cards for the sounds you have chosen to use

- First, check that they know the sound each letter makes and practise saying them together a few times.
- Explain that you have got some pictures that start with those sounds, but they are all mixed up.
- The children are going to help you sort them out. You will name each picture and the children will decide which letter it needs to go on.
- Give each child a turn at listening to a word and putting it on a letter until all the pictures are sorted correctly.
- When you have the piles of pictures, take it in turns to say each picture with the right sound.

Step down
○ Say the pictures together as a group.

Step up
○ Mix together all four sets of pictures (t/ck/d/g).

RHYME IT:
RHYME MATCH: OWN MODEL ACTIVITY ONE

What you need:
- Rhyming rule card (Resource 3)
- One and two syllable rhyming pictures (Resource 4)

- Remind the children of the rhyming rule 'the first sound is different but the rest is the same'. The children will complete this activity individually rather than at the same time.
- Give the children two pictures that don't rhyme. Make sure that one of the pair is a two syllable word and the other has only one syllable, e.g. 'coat' and 'flower'.
- Explain that you are going to give the children a picture that rhymes with one of the words, and they have to name each picture carefully and decide for themselves which two pictures rhyme.
- If they get it right, then they win the pair.

Step down
○ Talk about the last sound in the target word and be explicit about listening for that sound.

Step up
○ See whether the children can do the task silently, just thinking about the words in their head instead of saying them out loud.

49

WEEK 19

LISTEN FOR IT: SAME OR DIFFERENT JUDGEMENT: MIDDLE SOUND – NONSENSE WORDS

What you need:
- Same/different cue card (Resource 21)
- Same/different judgement word list – middle sound, nonsense words (Resource 22)
- Counters or similar

- Explain that you are going to say two nonsense words. They might be exactly the same or the middle sound might be different, e.g. 'bep' and 'bep' or 'zick' and 'zack'. The children will complete this activity individually rather than at the same time.
- The children have to listen carefully and if they think the words are the same, they put their counter on the 'same' card. If they think the words are different, then they put their counter on the 'different' card.
- Try the first one together so that the whole group can decide.
- Then let each child have an individual turn.

Step down
○ Use the step down long vowels word list (Resource 22)

Step up
○ Only give the children one chance to hear the pair of words.
○ Don't tell the children where in the word the sound might be different, e.g. beginning/middle/end.

CLAP IT: SYLLABLE DOMINOES

What you need:
- Syllable dominoes (Resource 24)

- Share the syllable dominoes out between all of the children and put one in the middle to start the game.
- Explain that they can only put pictures next to each other if they have the same number of claps, e.g. 'dog' can go next to 'cat' because the both have one clap.
- Clap out the two pictures on the first domino together and decide how many claps they both have.
- Choose someone to have the first turn. They have to look at their dominoes, and choose a picture that has the same number of claps as one of the starter domino pictures.
- The first child should put their picture down and the next child takes a turn.
- If a child does not have a domino with the right number of claps, they miss that turn.
- The winner is the first child to put all their pictures down.

Step down
○ Clap the pictures at the end of the domino chain each time so the children know the number of syllables they need to look for.

Step up
○ If they cannot go, encourage children to think of another word for one of their pictures to get the right number of syllables, e.g. if they need a three clap word, they can say 'space rocket' instead of 'rocket' so they don't miss their turn.

SAY IT:
SORT AND SAY: GLIDE SOUNDS

What you need:
- Initial sound pictures (Resource 14) that start with 'l' and 'w'
- Corresponding letter cards for these sounds

- Check that the children know the sound each letter makes and practise saying them together a few times.
- Then explain that you have got some pictures of words that start with those sounds, but they are all mixed up.
- The children are going to help you sort them out. You will say each picture and the children will decide which letter it needs to go on.
- Give each child a turn at listening to a word and putting it on a letter until all the pictures are sorted correctly.
- When you have the piles of pictures, take it in turns to say each word with the right sound.

Step down
○ Say the words together as a group.

Step up
○ Cover your mouth while you say the words so the children just have to listen to the sounds.

RHYME IT:
RHYME MATCH: OWN MODEL ACTIVITY TWO

What you need:
- Rhyming rule card (Resource 3)
- One syllable rhyming pictures (Resource 4)

- Remind the children of the rhyming rule 'the first sound is different but the rest is the same'. The children will complete this activity individually rather than at the same time.
- Give the children two pictures that don't rhyme. This time, make sure both words in the pair only have one syllable.
- Explain that you are going to give the children a picture that rhymes with one of the words, and they have to name each picture carefully and decide for themselves which two pictures rhyme. If they get it right, they win the pair.

Step down
○ Talk about the last sound in the target word and be explicit about listening for that sound.

Step up
○ See whether the children can do the task silently, just thinking about the words in their head instead of saying them out loud.

WEEK 20

LISTEN FOR IT: IS MY SOUND IN THE WORD?

What you need:
- 'Is my sound in the word?' list of words (Resource 25)
- Assign a target letter from the word list to each child
- Yes/no cards (Resource 12)
- Counters

- The children will complete this activity individually rather than at the same time.
- Give each child a letter from the alphabet and check that they know the sound it makes.
- Explain that you are going to say some words. The children have to listen carefully and decide whether they can hear their sound in the word.
- If the children think they can hear their sound, they need to put their counter on the 'yes' card. If not, then their counter should go on the 'no' card.
- Change the word for each child.

Step down
- If a child is finding this challenging give them longer sounds which are easier to hear such as 's' and 'f'.

Step up
- Choose one word for the whole group and if they hear their sound they have to stand up. If they are right they win a counter.

CLAP IT: ADD A SYLLABLE: THREE SYLLABLE WORDS

What you need:
- Three syllable picture cards (Resource 7)

- The children will complete this activity individually rather than at the same time.
- Explain to the children that you have lots of picture of words that all have three claps (syllables) in them, but you are not going to show the pictures. The children will need to guess what is on the picture by hearing the first two claps.
- You are only going to say the first two syllables for each picture, and the children will have to say the last syllable to win the picture.
- Try the first one together: say 'e –le –' and see whether the children can say 'phant' to complete the word and win the picture.
- Change the word for each child.

Step down
- Use pictures where the final clap is a real word. For example: 'ice cream van' or 'butterfly'.

Step up
- Use words where the final clap is not a real word. For example: 'grasshopper' or 'ambulance'.

SAY IT: SORT AND SAY: NOISY AND QUIET SOUNDS

What you need:
- Initial sound pictures (Resource 14) that start with: 't' and 'd' or 'k' and 'g'
- Letter cards

- Lay out the letter cards: 't' and 'd' or 'k' and 'g'.
- Check that the children know the sound each letter makes and practise saying the letters together a few times.
- Explain that you have lots of pictures of words that start with different letters (sounds) but they are all mixed up.
- The children will help you sort out the pictures. You will name each picture and the children will decide which letter it needs to go on. Say the word for each picture and the children will decide which letter card it needs to go on.
- Give each child a turn at listening to a word and putting it on a letter card until all the pictures are sorted correctly.
- When you have the piles of pictures, take it in turns to say each picture with the correct sound.

Step down
○ Say the pictures together as a group.

Step up
○ Mix together all sets of pictures.

RHYME IT: RHYMING RUNAROUND ACTIVITY TWO

What you need:
- Two sets of yes/no cards (Resource 12)
- Rhyming pictures (Resource 4)
- Rhyme judgement pictures (Resource 17)

- Explain that you have lots of pictures of words, some of them rhyme but some don't. You are going to give the children two pictures, and they have to say them out loud and decide whether they rhyme or not. The children will complete this activity individually rather than at the same time.
- Put out one set of 'yes' and 'no' cards at opposite sides of the room and keep one set for yourself.
- Explain that if the pictures rhyme, the children will need to run to the 'yes' card but if they don't they will run to the 'no' card.
- Choose two pictures, give them to the children and ask them to say the word out loud.
- Countdown 'three, two, one, go' and the children need to run to the 'yes' or the 'no' card.
- Once the children have run to the card, the adult shows them their own 'yes' or 'no' card so that they can check if they were right.
- Give each child a turn. If you would prefer to keep the activity table based then try giving each child a counter to put on the 'yes' or 'no' card instead.

Step down
○ Play it as a group activity so the children always have a model to copy.

Step up
○ See whether the children can do the task silently, just thinking of the words in their head instead of saying them out loud.

WEEK 21

LISTEN FOR IT: WHERE IN THE WORD: BEGINNING OR END

What you need:
- Sequencing caterpillar (Resource 5): 2 segments
- Initial sound pictures (Resource 14) and final sound pictures (Resource 18).
- Letter cards that correspond to the sounds used in the pictures

- The children will complete this activity individually rather than at the same time.
- Select an assortment of focus letters and check that the children know the sound that each letter makes. For example, '/c/'.
- Explain that you have lots of pictures of words that have different sounds at the start and end of the word.
- The aim is for the children to identify where each sound is in each word: at the beginning or at the end. They will use the sequencing caterpillar to show where the sound is.
- Name a picture that has the focus sound within it. The child has to decide whether the focus sound is at the beginning or end of the word.
- If the child thinks they can hear the sound at the beginning, they put the letter on the caterpillar's head. If they think it is at the end then they put it on the caterpillar's tail.

Step down
- Work as a group to identify the sound in each picture.

Step up
- Give everyone a different letter and corresponding set of pictures to listen for.

CLAP IT: ADD A SYLLABLE: TWO SYLLABLE WORDS

What you need:
- Syllable picture cards (Resource 7): two syllable words

- The children will complete this activity individually rather than at the same time.
- Explain that you have some pictures of words that have two claps (syllables) in them, but you are not going to show them to the children.
- You are only going to say the first clap and the children have to say the last clap to win the picture.
- Try the first one together. Say 'bis –' and see whether the children can say '– cuit' to complete the word and win the picture.
- Change the word for each child.

Step down
- Give the children a clue about what the word might be, e.g. 'it's something you eat and the first clap is...'

Step up
- Use the 'add a syllable' step up pictures (Resource 26) for two syllable words, using new vocabulary.

SAY IT:
REAL WORD OR NOT: VOWEL-CONSONANT (VC) WORDS

What you need:
- Sequencing caterpillar (Resource 5): two segments
- Real and nonsense VC words (Resource 28)

- Explain that you are going to make some two letter words on the sequencing caterpillar. The children will have to read the word out loud and decide whether it is a real word or not.
- Ask the children to close their eyes whilst you make the first word on the caterpillar, e.g. 'up'.
- Everyone opens their eyes and reads it together. The children give you a thumbs up if it is a real word and thumbs down if not.

Step down
○ Don't ask children to close their eyes. Let them watch you while you say each sound as you make the word.

Step up
○ Change both the vowel and the consonant each time you make a new word.

RHYME IT:
RHYMING: ODD ONE OUT ACTIVITY ONE

What you need:
- Rhyming rule card (Resource 3)
- Rhyming pictures (Resource 4)

- The children will complete this activity individually rather than at the same time.
- Remind the children of the rhyming rule: the first sound is different but the rest is the same.
- Put out three pictures (two that rhyme and one that doesn't rhyme). Explain that two of the pictures will rhyme and one of them does not.
- The child names each picture and decides which one does not rhyme.
- Change the pictures for each child.
- Make sure that the non-rhyming picture is in a different place in the sequence each time.

Step down
○ Name the pictures for the children.

Step up
○ See whether the children can do the task independently, thinking of the words in their head instead of saying them out loud.

WEEK 22

 LISTEN FOR IT:
WHERE IN THE WORD: BEGINNING, MIDDLE OR END

What you need:
- Sequencing caterpillar (Resource 5): 3 segments
- Where in the word? (Resource 27)
- Letter cards that correspond to your chosen sound

- Select a letter from the 'where in the word' list. Show the children the letter and check that they know the sound it makes.
- Explain that you are going to say some words that have that sound at the beginning, middle or end.
- The children have to decide where in the word the target sound is, using the sequencing caterpillar to show this.
- Say a word and if the children think they can hear the sound at the beginning, they put the letter on the caterpillar's head. If they think it is in the middle, they put the letter on the caterpillar's tummy. If they think it is at the end, they put it on the caterpillar's tail.
- Repeat the process with a different word but using the same letter.

Step down
- Focus on letters appearing at the start and end of words.
- Say the word one syllable at a time so it is easier to hear the sound.

Step up
- Give each child a different letter to listen for.

 CLAP IT:
SYLLABLE TAKEAWAY: PREFIXES AND SUFFIXES

What you need:
- Word takeaway lists (Resource 16)

- The children will complete this activity individually rather than at the same time.
- Choose some two syllable words from the word takeaway list.
- Explain that you are going to say a two clap (syllable) word and then ask the children to take away either the first or the last clap.
- Do the first one together, e.g. 'You need to take the last clap away from the word 'spider'. What word are we left with when we take away 'der'?'
- Change the word for each child.

Step down
- Repeat the word leaving a small gap between the syllables e.g. 'care – less'.
- If a child is finding this challenging, focus on the suffix list of words, always taking away the last clap.

Step up
- Vary between asking the child to take away the first or the last clap.

SAY IT:
REAL WORD OR NOT: CVC WORDS

What you need:
- Sequencing caterpillar (Resource 5): three segments
- Real and nonsense words (Resource 28)

- Remind children about how to use the sequencing caterpillar to help sound out words: they are going stroke the caterpillar whilst saying the sounds to make the word.
- Explain that you are going to make some three letter words on the caterpillar. The children will have to read the word and decide whether it is a real word or not.
- Ask the children to close their eyes whilst you make the first word on the caterpillar, e.g. 'bat'.
- Ask everyone to open their eyes and read the word out together. The children give you a thumbs up if it is a real word, and thumbs down if not.
- Once they are confident, give each child a turn individually.

Step down
○ Don't ask the children to close their eyes. Get them to watch you say each sound as you make the new word.

Step up
○ Change all three letters each time you make a new word.

RHYME IT:
RHYMING: ODD ONE OUT ACTIVITY TWO

What you need:
- Rhyming rule card (Resource 3)
- Rhyme judgement pictures (Resource 17)

- Use the rhyming rule card to remind children about the rules for rhyming words. Explain that you are going to play the same odd one out game (from week 21), but this week the words will sound almost the same and you are not going to say the words out loud for them.
- Put out three pictures from the rhyme judgement pictures. Explain that two of the pictures rhyme, and one of them does not, e.g. 'duck, snake, cake'.
- Ask the children to say the words for each picture out loud. Can they spot the odd one out?
- Repeat with new pictures, making sure that the odd picture appears in a different place in the sequence each time.

Step down
○ Talk about the middle sound in each word and be explicit about listening for that sound.

Step up
○ See whether the children can do the task independently, thinking about the words in their head instead of saying them out loud.

WEEK 23

LISTEN FOR IT: WHICH ONE IS RIGHT?

What you need:
- Choose a set of initial sound pictures (Resource 14)
- Choose sounds that need additional practise within your group

- Choose a picture from the initial sound pictures cards. Show the children and explain that you are going to say the word in lots of different ways but that only one way will be right.
- Ask the children to give you a thumbs down if you get the word wrong. Ask them to give you a thumbs up when they hear you say the word correctly.
- Say the word with lots of different initial sounds. For example: if 'sun' is your chosen word, you might say 'dun', 'yun', 'tun' and 'sun'.
- Pause after each time you say the word to allow the children to give you a thumbs up or thumbs down.

Step down
- Exaggerate the initial sound each time you say it to make it easier for the children to hear.

Step up
- Leave shorter pauses after saying each word and get the children to respond with a thumbs up or thumbs down as you are talking.
- If you have children in your group who consistently substitute a sound (for example, they always use 'd' for 's'), include their substitution as one of the incorrect pronunciations.

CLAP IT: WHICH ONE AM I THINKING ABOUT ACTIVITY ONE

What you need:
- One, two and three syllable pictures (Resource 7): choose pictures from one topic, e.g. minibeasts

- Choose three pictures from the same topic that each have one, two and three syllables, e.g. minibeasts. Put them out in front of the children and make sure they know the words for the pictures.
- Explain that you are thinking about one of the pictures but you are not going to tell the children which one it is. You are going to give them a clue by clapping the word.
- The children will need to guess which picture you are thinking of based on the number of claps, e.g. for 'worm', 'beetle' and 'dragonfly', you could clap three times. The children will need to count the number of claps and connect that to 'dragonfly'.

Step down
- Just use a one and three syllable picture to make the contrast easier to hear.
- Clap the pictures together before beginning the guessing activity.

Step up
- Don't clap the word but just say how many syllables it has. For example: 'I am thinking of a three-clap word'.

SAY IT:
SORT AND SAY: LONG AND SHORT SOUNDS

What you need:
- Initial sound pictures (Resource 14) that start with either: 's' and 'd' or 'f' and 'b'
- Letter cards that correspond to the sounds and pictures you have chosen

- Lay out the letter cards for 's', 'd', 'f' and 'b'. Check that the children know the sound each letter makes and practise saying them together a few times.
- Explain that you have some pictures of words that start with those sounds but they are all mixed up.
- The children are going to help you sort out the pictures. You will name each word and the children will decide which letter the picture needs to go on.
- Give each child a turn, listening to a word and putting it on a letter until all the pictures have been sorted correctly.
- When you have four piles of 's', 'd', 'f' and 'b' pictures, make the game harder by mixing up the sets again.
- Get the children to take it in turns to say each picture and remember which sound to use, pointing to the correct letter card each time.
- If they say the word with the right sound, they win the picture.

Step down
○ Say the pictures together as a group.

Step up
○ Mix together all four sets of pictures (s/d/f/b).

RHYME IT:
RHYMING PAIRS

What you need:
- Rhyming pictures (Resource 4). You will need a pair of rhyming pictures for each child in your group, e.g. if you have six children, choose six pairs.

- Put pairs of rhyming pictures out on the table, face up.
- Explain that everyone is going to have a turn finding two pictures that rhyme.
- If they are correct, they win the pair.

Step down
○ Give one picture to each child rather than placing all the pictures on the table. They will then only have to look for their own rhyming picture from the six left on the table.

Step up
○ Turn over the pictures so that they are face down. The children then have to turn two over, check whether they rhyme and turn them back over if not. The group then has to remember where those pictures are so that they can make a pair.

WEEK 24

LISTEN FOR IT:
SPOT THE ERROR: INITIAL SOUNDS CHOICE OF SIX

What you need:
- Initial sound pictures (Resource 14)
- Choose letters or sounds that need additional practise within your group

- Explain that you are going to put six pictures out and name, them but you will name one wrong.
- The children have to listen carefully and say 'stop!' when they hear you make a mistake.
- Pick six pictures that all start with the same sound.
- Say the words for the children using the wrong first sound for one of the words. For example: 'fish, fire, four, binger, foot, five'.
- The children should tell you to stop when they hear you say 'binger'.

Step down
- Repeat the sequence much more slowly, emphasising the initial sounds.

Step up
- Explain that this time, you are going to make two mistakes; the children must wait until you have named all of the pictures before telling you which two were wrong.
- Ask the children to tell you the correct way to say the words.

CLAP IT:
WHICH ONE AM I THINKING ABOUT ACTIVITY TWO

What you need:
- Once, two, three and four syllable pictures (Resource 7): pictures from one topic, e.g. transport

- Choose four pictures from the same topic that each have one, two, three and four syllables. Put them out in front of the children. Make sure the children know the names of the pictures.
- Explain that you are thinking about one of the pictures, but you are not going to tell the children which one it is.
- You are going to give the children a clue by clapping the word.
- Clap the syllables of a picture without naming it, e.g. if you have 'bike', 'rocket', 'ambulance' and 'helicopter', you could clap four times. The children will need to count the number of claps and connect that to 'helicopter'.

Step down
- Just use a one and four syllable picture to make the contrast easier to hear.
- Clap the pictures together before beginning the guessing activity.

Step up
- Don't clap the word but just say how many syllables it has, e.g. 'I am thinking of a three clap word'.

SAY IT:
SORT AND SAY: MIXED UP FRONT AND BACK SOUNDS

What you need:
- Initial sound pictures (Resource 14) that start with either: 't' and 'k' or 'd' and 'g'
- Two sets of letter cards that correspond to the sounds and pictures you have chosen.

- Lay out letter cards for 't', 'k', 'd' and 'g'. Check that the children know the sound each letter makes and practise saying them together a few times.
- Explain that you have lots of pictures of words that start with t /k /d /g sounds, but that they are all mixed up. The children are going to help you sort them out.
- Name each picture and the children will decide which letter it needs to go on. Specify if you are looking for the start sound or the end sound.
- Give each child a turn, listening to a word and putting it on the corresponding first letter until all the pictures have been sorted.
- When you have two piles of pictures, make it harder by mixing up the two sets again. Then they will take it in turns to say each picture and see whether they can remember which sound to use. If they get the word right, then they win the picture.

Step down
- Say the pictures together as a group.
- Focus on just two sounds at a time before introducing more.

Step up
- Mix together all four sets of pictures (t/ck/d/g)

RHYME IT:
COLLECTING RHYMES

What you need:
- Rhyming pictures (Resource 4). You will need a set for each child in your group, so if you have six children choose six sets.

- Give each child one picture from the rhyme pictures cards and hide their pair cards around the room.
- Explain that when you say 'go', the children need to look for two more pictures that rhyme with theirs.
- The first person to find their rhymes is the winner.
- Repeat the game giving each child a new starter picture.
- This game can be played as a table top activity too.

Step down
- Let the children work in pairs.
- Name the rhyming sets together before starting the activity.

Step up
- Time how long it takes for everyone to find their rhyming picture. See if they can beat their last score with a new set of rhymes.

WEEK 25

LISTEN FOR IT: SPOT THE ERROR: NO FINAL SOUND

What you need:
- Final sound pictures (Resource 18)

- Put out three pictures from the final sound pictures, and explain that you will name each picture but you will miss off the end sound for one of the pictures.
- Ask the children to listen carefully and say 'stop!' when they hear you miss the end sound for a word.
- Pick three words that end with the same sound and say the words to the children, but on one word miss off the final sound, e.g. if you choose 'f' as the end of word sound, you might say 'knife, roof, lea_'.
- Ask the children to tell you which word is missing the final sound.

Step down
- Give the children the final letter/sound they are listening out for, e.g. 'these pictures all end with a 's' sound but I am going to miss the sound on one picture – can you spot which one?'

Step up
- Use sets of pictures with different final sounds.
- Ask the children to tell you how you should have said the word?

CLAP IT: I SPY CLAPPING ONE, TWO AND THREE CLAPS

What you need:
- One, two and three syllable pictures (Resource 7): pictures from two topics, e.g. food and animals
- Syllable clap cards (Resource 1)

- Put the one, two and three syllable pictures around the room.
- Explain that you are going to show the children a clap card. When you say 'go', they need to find a picture with that number of claps in it, e.g. if you show them a two clap card they might bring back the picture of a monkey.
- Clap out the words as the children bring the pictures back to you to check that they were right.
- This game can be played as a table top activity too.

Step down
- Clap the words together as you set them out before beginning the activity.
- Let children work in pairs.

Step up
- Divide the children into teams and see which team is the fastest at finding pictures.

SAY IT:
SORT AND SAY: MIXED UP GLIDE SOUNDS

What you need:
- Initial sound pictures (Resource 14) that start with 'l' and 'w'
- Letter cards that correspond to the sounds and pictures you have chosen

- Lay out the letter cards for 'l' and 'w'. Check that the children know the sound each letter makes and practise saying them together a few times.
- Explain that you have some pictures that start with those sounds, but they are all mixed up.
- The children help you sort out the pictures. You will name each word and the children will decide which letter it needs to go on.
- Give each child a turn at listening to a word and putting it on a letter until all the pictures have been sorted correctly.
- When you have two piles of 'l' and 'w' pictures, mix the two sets up again.
- Get the children to take it in turns to say each picture and remember which sound to use.

Step down
○ Say the words together as a group.

Step up
○ Cover your mouth while you say the words so the children just have to listen.

RHYME IT:
ANIMAL PICNIC RHYMING PAIRS

What you need:
- Animal picnic game cards (Resource 9)

- Put the pictures of animals and their rhyming foods from the animal picnic game cards out on the table, face up.
- Explain that everyone is going to have a turn matching an animal with the rhyming food they like to eat, e.g. 'Harry horse eats sauce'.
- The children take it in turns to first choose an animal, and then choose a food that they think rhymes with their animal.
- If they are right then they win the pair.

Step down
○ Choose an animal picture from each pair and give one to each child so that they only have to look for the rhyming food.

Step up
○ See whether the children can find the rhyming pictures silently.

WEEK 26

 LISTEN FOR IT: SORTING FINAL SOUND OR NO FINAL SOUND

What you need:
- Final sound/no final sound picture cards (Resource 29)
- Tail, no tail picture card (Resource 29)

- Put out the tail/no tail picture card.
- Explain that you have a selection of pictures. Some have a sound at the end, e.g. 'cake', and some do not, e.g. 'key'.
- Ask the children to listen carefully and help you sort the pictures into the two categories: final sound or no final sound.
- If they can hear a sound at the end, they put the picture on the dog with a tail. If there is no sound at the end, they put it on the dog with no tail.
- Do the first one together as a group and then give each child a turn.

Step down
○ Repeat the word multiple times and break it into segments so they can hear the individual sounds.

Step up
○ Give the children the picture first and see whether they can name it themselves before putting it on the right card.

 CLAP IT: TRICKY WORD CLAPPING

What you need:
- Two, three and four syllable clap cards (Resource 1)
- Tricky syllable picture cards (Resource 30)

- Explain that you have some tricky words to clap. Children sometimes miss out a clap when they say these words. For example, they say 'nana' when they mean 'banana'.
- Explain to the children that they are going to clap out the words and decide how many claps each word should have. Then you are going to say them with the right number of claps.
- Do the first one together, e.g. 'sa – fa – ri'. Clap out the syllables together and decide which clap card it needs to go on.
- Say it together, touching the clap card as you say each syllable to check you are right.
- Give each child a turn, going through all of the tricky words on the cards.

Step down
○ Continue clapping the words as a group.

Step up
○ Once the children have sorted all the pictures, mix them up again and see whether they can still remember how to say them.

SAY IT:
CONSONANT-CONSONANT-VOWEL-CONSONANT (CCVC) BLENDING: GLIDE SOUNDS

What you need:
- Sequencing caterpillar (Resource 5): 4 segments
- CCVC word list (Resource 31)
- Letter cards that correspond to the sounds and pictures on the CCVC word list

- Explain that you are going to make some long words on the sequencing caterpillar. Each word will be four letters long.
- Explain that you are going to stroke each part of the caterpillar while you say the sounds that make up the word. You always need to stroke the caterpillar in the same direction, starting at the head and continuing until you complete the word.
- Make a word on the caterpillar, putting one letter card in each segment.
- Say the word together, stroking the caterpillar as you say the sounds, modelling how to keep the sounds going so that they blend into each other, e.g. 'flap'.
- Make a new word on the caterpillar and let each child have a turn at reading it as they stroke the sounds on the caterpillar.

Step down
- Continue 'reading' the four-letter words as a group.
- Let the children watch you making the word, one sound at a time, saying the sound as you put each letter card onto the caterpillar.
- If a child finds it challenging, only change the initial sound each time. For example, if the previous child had 'flap' then just change the first sound to make 'slap'.

Step up
- Change all of the sounds in the word each time so the child has to blend all four sounds.

RHYME IT:
RHYME AROUND THE CIRCLE: NO LETTER CLUES

What you need:
- Rhyming rule card (Resource 3)
- Rhyming pictures (Resource 4)
- Counts or similar
- A timer or stopwatch for the step up activity

- Get everyone to sit in a circle. Explain that the children are going to see how many rhyming words they can think of for each picture on the rhyme picture cards. The rhymes can be real words or nonsense words.
- Good rhyming words for this game include: 'cat', 'key', 'shoe', 'chair', 'bed' and 'car'.
- Choose a rhyming picture to start the circle, e.g. 'bear'. Show the picture to the group and say a word that rhymes, e.g. 'chair'.
- Pass the picture around the circle. If the child can think of a rhyme they win a counter and pass the picture on. If the child can't think of a rhyme they just pass the picture on.
- Once the picture has been all the way around the circle, choose a new picture.
- The winner is the person with the most counters at the end of the game.

Step down
- Give the child a letter to help them think of a rhyming word.

Step up
- Use a timer or stopwatch to record how long it takes to make all of the new rhyming words. See if the children can beat their time with each new picture.

WEEK 27

LISTEN FOR IT: SORTING 'L' BLENDS

What you need:
- One and two cards (Resource 32)
- 'l' blend minimal pairs cards (Resource 33)
- Letter card 'l'

- Put out the one and two number cards.
- Explain that you have some pictures of words. Some have two sounds at the start and some only have one. Give the children an example, e.g. 'back' starts with one sound and 'black' starts with two.
- Ask the children to listen carefully as you name two pictures from the 'l' blend minimal pairs card.
- They need to put the picture with two sounds at the start on the number two card. The picture with just one sound at the start will go on the number one card.
- Do the first pair together, and then give each child a turn with a new pair of pictures.

Step down
- Put the 'l' letter card next to the two card so they know which sound to listen for.

Step up
- Present pictures one at a time instead of as a pair and see if the child can decide whether it goes on the number one or two card.

CLAP IT: SPOT THE ERROR: SYLLABLES

What you need:
- Three and four syllable picture cards (Resource 7)

- Explain that you are going to put three pictures out and name them, but you will get one wrong.
- Ask the children to listen carefully and say 'stop!' when they hear you make a mistake.
- Pick three words with three or four syllables. Say the words but for one of the words, miss out a syllable from the middle, e.g. 'am – bu – lance', 'but – fly' and 'ba – na – na'.
- See if the children can identify which word has the missing syllable.

Step down
- Take one picture away so they only have to listen to two words, and decide which was wrong.

Step up
- Ask the children to name the picture correctly.

SAY IT: WHAT'S THE NEW WORD ACTIVITY ONE

What you need:
- What's the new word? (Resource 34): week 27 column
- Letter cards: 'b', 'c', 'f', 'g', 'j', 'l', 'm' and 'n'

- Explain that you are going to say a word and give the children a letter. They need to add the letter to make a new word and tell you what the new word is.
- Say the first word on the 'what's the new word' card list: 'imp', and choose the letter to go with it: 'l'.
- Ask 'what do you get if you add 'l' to imp?' and see whether the children can tell you the new word: 'limp'.
- Give each child a turn with a new word and letter.

Step down
- Say the letter sound rather than the letter name.
- Remind children that the letter will be added to the beginning of the word.

Step up
- Find different letters that you can add to make more new words, e.g. digraphs: 'ch' and 'sh'.

RHYME IT: PEOPLE PICNIC GAME

What you need:
- People picnic game cards (Resource 35)

- Using the people picnic game cards, explain that the characters are going on a picnic but all their food has been mixed up.
- The children need to help by matching the food to the correct character, but the characters only eat foods that rhyme with their name, e.g. 'Molly' and 'lolly'.
- Put out all the food and character pictures, naming them with the children.
- Choose a character and say their name out loud.
- Choose three food pictures (including the target rhyme) and say each food with the character's name to allow the child to hear whether they rhyme or not. For example: 'Luna, what does she like? Luna, ham, Luna, tuna, Luna, melon?'.

Step down
- Stick to a choice of two foods, the target rhyme and one other.

Step up
- Don't give a choice of foods. Instead, put all the food cards on the table and see whether the children can find the right one.

WEEK 28

LISTEN FOR IT: SORTING 'S' BLENDS

What you need:
- One and two cards (Resource 32)
- 's' blend minimal pairs cards (Resource 36)

- Put out the one and two number cards.
- Explain that you have some pictures. Some have two sounds at the start and some have one, e.g. 'snail' has two sounds and 'nail' has one.
- Ask the children to listen carefully as you name two pictures from the 's' blend minimal pairs card.
- The children need to put the picture with two sounds at the start on the number two card. The picture with just one sound at the start will go on the number one card.
- Do the first pair together, and then give each child a turn with a new pair of pictures.

Step down
- Put a letter 's' next to the number two card so the children know which sound to listen for.

Step up
- Present pictures one at a time instead of as a pair and see if the child can decide whether it goes on the number one or two card.

CLAP IT: SYLLABLE RACE

What you need:
- One, two, three and four syllable pictures. Choose pictures from two topics, e.g. food and animals. (Resource 7)
- One, two, three and four syllable clap cards. If you have more than four children in your group, you will need two sets (Resource 1)

- Put the one, two, three and four syllable pictures face up on the table.
- Explain that you are going to give everyone a different number clap card. When you say 'go', they all need to find a picture with that number of claps (syllables) in it. For example, if they have a two clap card, they will each have to find a two clap word, e.g. 'tractor'.
- The first person to find a picture with the right number of claps wins that picture.

Step down
- Clap the pictures together as you set them out before beginning the activity.
- Reduce the number of pictures to choose from.

Step up
- See whether the children can do the activity independently without saying the word out loud.
- Change the syllable number they are listening for each time.

SAY IT: WHAT'S THE NEW WORD ACTIVITY TWO

What you need:
- What's the new word? card (Resource 34): week 28 column
- Consonant blends: 'bl', 'pl', 'sw', 'cl', 'st', 'sl', 'fl', 'pr', 'sm' (Resource 43)

- Explain that you are going to say a word and give the children two letters. They need to add the two letters to make a new word and tell you what the new word is.
- Say the first word on the 'what's the new word' card list: 'imp', and choose the blended two letters to go with it: 'bl'.
- Ask 'what do you get if you add 'bl' to imp?' and see whether the children can tell you the new word: 'blimp'.
- Give each child a turn with a new word and two letters.

Step down
○ Continue to work as a group.
○ Use pictures as visuals and write out the words to show children the sounds.

Step up
○ Give children the letter blend without saying it for them.

RHYME IT: WIN THE PICTURE: NO CLUES

What you need:
- Rhyming rule card (Resource 3)
- Rhyming pictures (Resource 4)

- Use the rhyming rule card to remind children about the rules for rhyming words.
- Explain that you are going to play the 'win the picture' game (from week one)
- Explain that you have lots of pictures and you are going to see if the children can win them from you by guessing what they are. They have to listen to your clues and see whether they can guess what your picture is. Explain that you will not say the name of the picture, but instead you will tell them what word it rhymes with and see whether they can guess what one you are thinking of.
- Lay out the rhyming pictures, keeping one of each rhyming pair for yourself and putting the other face up on the table.
- Choose one of your pictures, for example 'snake'. Don't let the children see your card.
- Say: 'I am thinking of the picture that rhymes with cake' and see whether they can find 'snake' on the table to win the pair.
- Give each child a turn with a new picture until all the pairs have been won.

Step down
○ Give them a semantic clue, for example: 'I am thinking of something that is an animal and rhymes with cake'.

Step up
○ Show them your picture but don't name the word and see if they can find the rhyming card on the table.

WEEK 29

LISTEN FOR IT: SORTING BLENDS: 'L' AND 'S' BLENDS

What you need:
- One and two cards (Resource 32)
- 'l' blend minimal pairs cards (Resource 33)
- 's' blend minimal pairs cards (Resource 36)

- Put out the one and two number cards.
- Explain that you have some pictures of words, some of which have two sounds at the start and some that only have one, e.g. 'black' has two sounds and 'back' has one.
- Mix up the 'l' blend and 's' blend minimal pairs cards.
- The children are going to listen carefully as you name a picture.
- If they think it has two sounds at the start, then they will put it on the number two card. If they think that it has one sound at the start then it will go on the number one card.
- Do the first picture together as a group and then give each child a turn with new pictures.

Step down
○ Use only one set of blend pictures, either 's' blend or 'l' blend pictures.

Step up
○ Show the children the picture without saying the name. See whether they can name it themselves and decide where it should go.

CLAP IT: ADD A SYLLABLE: MAKE A WORD

What you need:
- Add a syllable, make a word list (Resource 37)
- Counters to win

- Explain that you are going to make some new words by adding two syllables together.
- Give the children a picture, e.g. 'key', and tell them a new syllable to add to it, e.g. 'don'. See if the children can create a new word: 'donkey'.
- Give each child a turn. For each new word, they win a counter.

Step down
○ Name the picture for the children and give the syllables in the right order, e.g. 'can you add 'don' to 'key'?'.

Step up
○ Ask the children to think of a different syllable to add to the word to win an extra counter, e.g. 'monkey' as well as 'donkey'.

SAY IT:
CONSONANT-CONSONANT-VOWEL-CONSONANT (CCVC) BLENDING: 'S' BLENDS

What you need:
- Sequencing caterpillar (Resource 5): 4 segments
- CCVC word list (Resource 31). Use the 's' blends column.
- Letter cards to match word list

- Explain that you are going to make some long words on the sequencing caterpillar. The children will need four letters to make the words and you will focus on 's' blending sounds.
- Explain that you are going to stroke each part of the caterpillar whilst you say the sounds to make the word.
- You always need to stroke the caterpillar in the same direction, starting at the head and continuing until you complete the word.
- Make a new word on the caterpillar, putting one letter in each segment. Say the word together, stroking the caterpillar as you say the sounds. Model how to keep the sounds going so that they blend into each other, e.g. 'step'.
- Make a new word on the caterpillar and let each child have a turn at reading it as they stroke the sounds on the caterpillar.

Step down
- Continue 'reading' the words as a group.
- Let the children watch you making the word, one sound at a time, saying the sound as you put it on the caterpillar.

Step up
- Add the 'l' blend words in too and see if the children can alternate between the two blends.

RHYME IT:
PEOPLE PICNIC RHYMING PAIRS

What you need:
- People picnic game cards (Resource 35)

- Put the characters and food from the people picnic game cards out on the table, face up.
- Explain that everyone needs to find a character and match them to the rhyming food that they like to eat, e.g. 'Kai' and 'pie'.
- The children take it in turns to choose a character and then choose a food that they think rhymes with the character's name.
- If they are right, they win that pair.

Step down
- Choose a character picture from each pair and give one to each child so that they only have to look for the rhyming food.

Step up
- See whether the children can find the rhyming pictures independently.

WEEK 30

LISTEN FOR IT: SORTING FINAL BLENDS: 'S' SOUNDS

What you need:
- One and two cards (Resource 32)
- Final blend minimal pairs cards (Resource 38)

- Put out the one and two number cards.
- Name all the pictures from the final blend minimal pairs cards with the children.
- Explain that you have some pictures of words, some have two sounds at the end and some have one sound at the end, e.g. 'nest' has two sounds at the end and 'net' has one.
- The children are going to listen carefully as you name a picture. If they think it has two sounds at the end then they will put it on the number two card. If they think that it has one sound at the end then it will go on the number one card.
- Do the first picture together as a group and then give each child a turn with new pictures.

Step down
- Present the pictures as a pair so it is easier to hear which one has the extra sound, e.g. 'vet' and 'vest'.

Step up
- Show the picture without saying the name. See whether the children can name it themselves and decide where it should go.

CLAP IT: ANCHOR WORDS

What you need:
- Anchor words and Step down clues (Resource 39)
- Counters

- Explain that you have some pictures of words that can be added to other words to make lots of new words.
- Give each child a picture and explain that they will win a counter for every new word that they can make. For example, if the anchor word is 'light' then they could make 'lighthouse', 'lightbulb', 'starlight'.
- If a child thinks of more than one new word, they earn an extra counter for each one.
- The game finishes when everyone has had a turn with their picture.

Step down
- Use step down clues to help children think of a new word.
- Continue to work as a group or work in pairs.

Step up
- Just use one picture at a time. Pass the picture to the first child. As soon as they have thought of a new word, they win a counter and pass on the picture. If a child can't think of a word then they just pass the picture on.

SAY IT:
CONSONANT-VOWEL-CONSONANT-CONSONANT (CVCC) BLENDING: FINAL BLEND WORDS

What you need:
- Sequencing caterpillar (Resource 5): 4 segments
- Final blend word list (CVCC words) (Resource 40)
- Letter cards that correspond to the sounds and pictures on the CVCC word list

- Explain that you are going to make some long words on the sequencing caterpillar. The children will need four letters to make the words.
- Remind the children that they need to stroke each part of the caterpillar whilst saying the sounds to make the word.
- You always need to stroke the caterpillar in the same direction, starting at the head and continuing until you complete the word. Then make a word on the sequencing caterpillar putting one letter in each segment. Say the word together, stroking the caterpillar as you say the sounds, modelling how to keep the sounds going so they blend into each other. For example: 'best'.
- Make a new word on the caterpillar, putting one letter in each segment. Say the word together, stroking the caterpillar as you say the sounds. Model how to keep the sounds going so that they blend into each other, e.g. 'best'

Step down
- Continue 'reading' the words as a group.
- Let the children watch you making the word, saying one sound at a time as you put it on the caterpillar.

Step up
- Change all of the sounds in the word so the children have to blend all four sounds.

RHYME IT:
RHYME WORKSHOP

What you need:
- Rhyme workshop cards (Resource 41)
- Letter cards

- Give the children a picture and tell them that they are going to make a new rhyme from it.
- They will need to take the first sound away and add two new sounds to make the new rhyme, e.g. if the picture is 'hat' and the new sound is /fl/, they can take the first sound away (/h/) and add on /fl/ to make the word 'flat'.
- Give each child a turn with a new picture.

Step down
- Split the word into segments, e.g. 'flat' is /fl/ and /at/. See whether the children can add the new sounds on to the second segment to make a new rhyme.

Step up
- Give the child a picture and the new letters. See whether they can independently take off the first sound and add the two new sounds.

RESOURCE 1

SYLLABLE CLAP CARDS

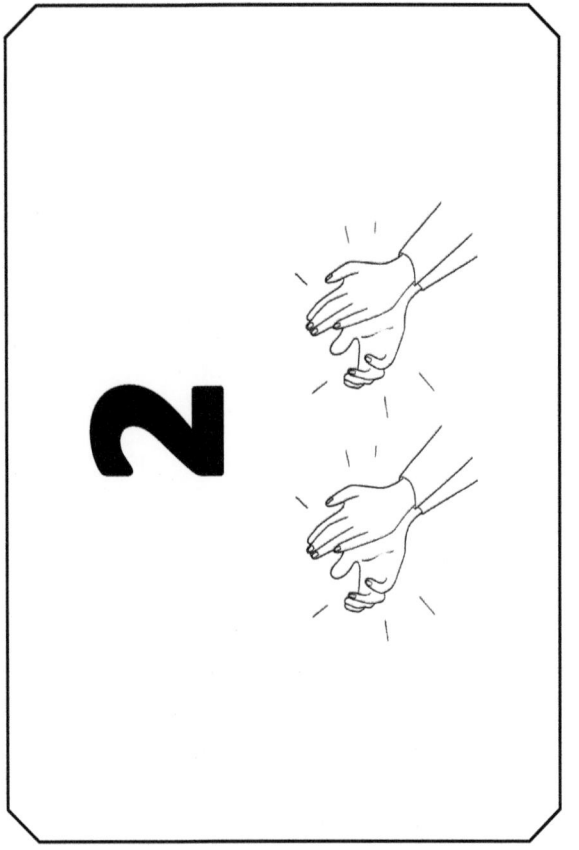

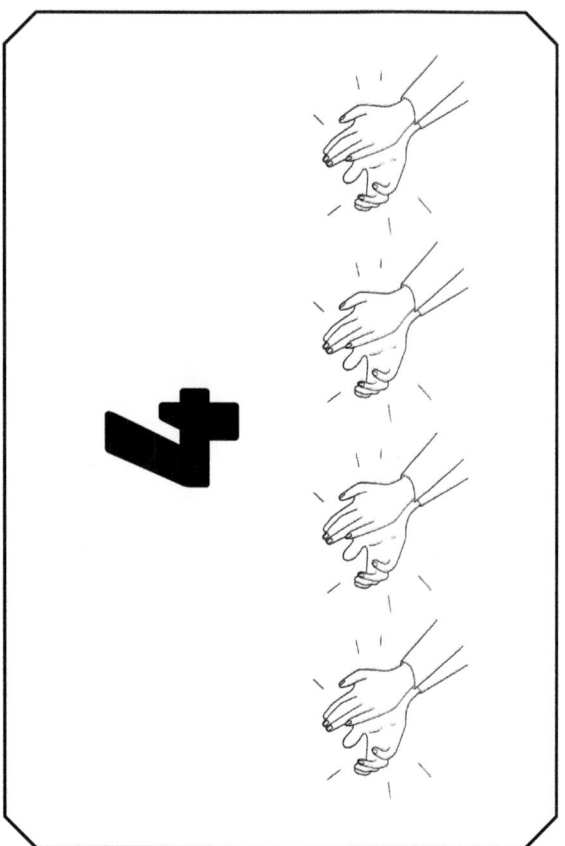

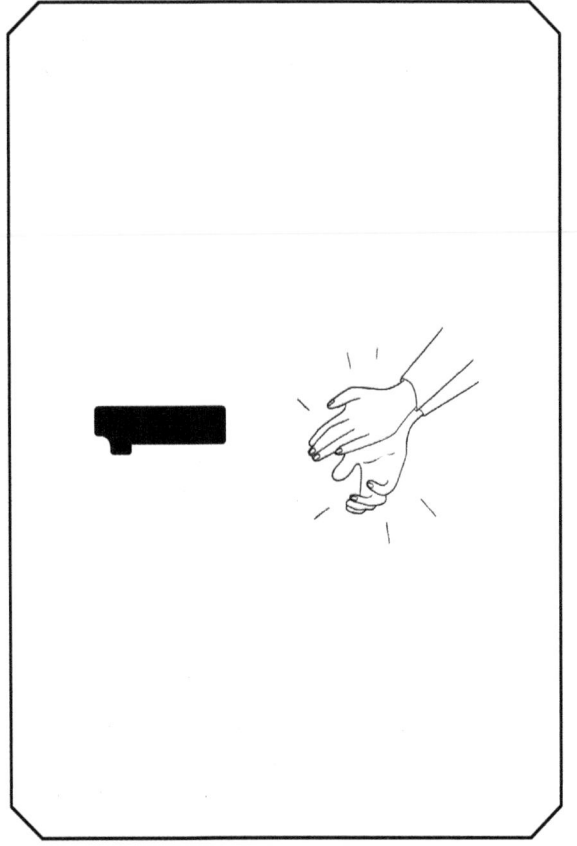

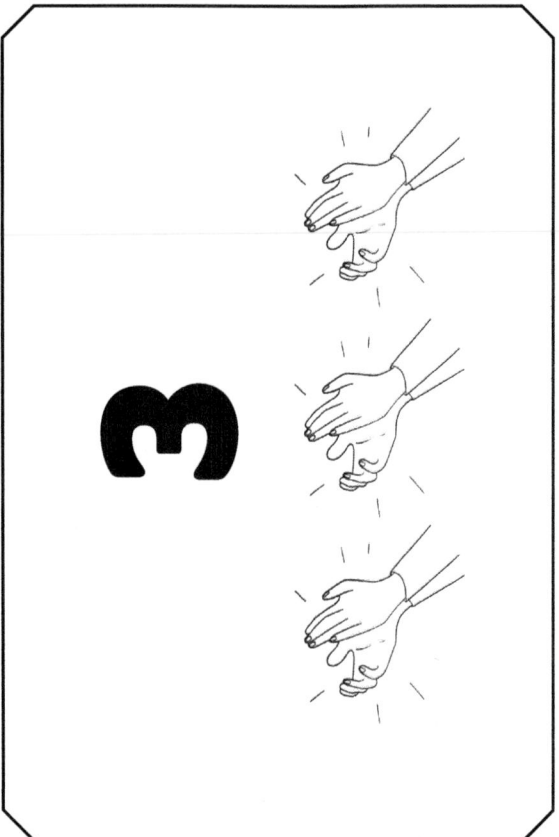

© Bloomsbury Education, 2026

RESOURCE 2

ANIMAL NOISES CARDS

© Bloomsbury Education, 2026

RHYMING RULE CARD

The Rhyme Rule

The first sound is <u>different</u>

The rest sounds the <u>same</u>

△ ○   ○ ○

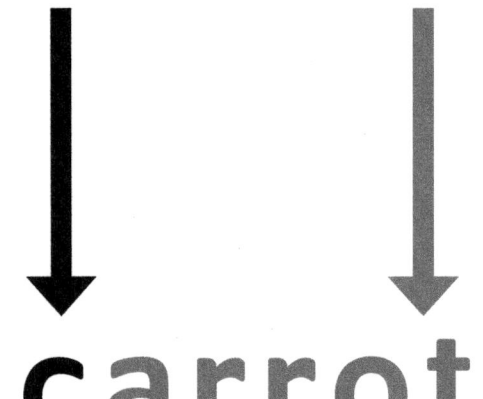

RHYMING PICTURES

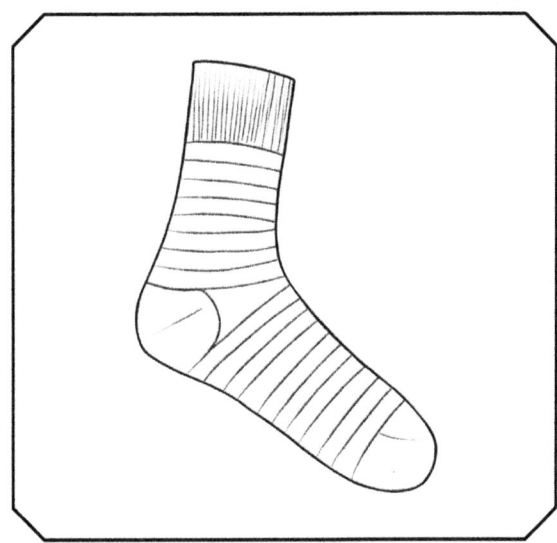

RHYMING PICTURES

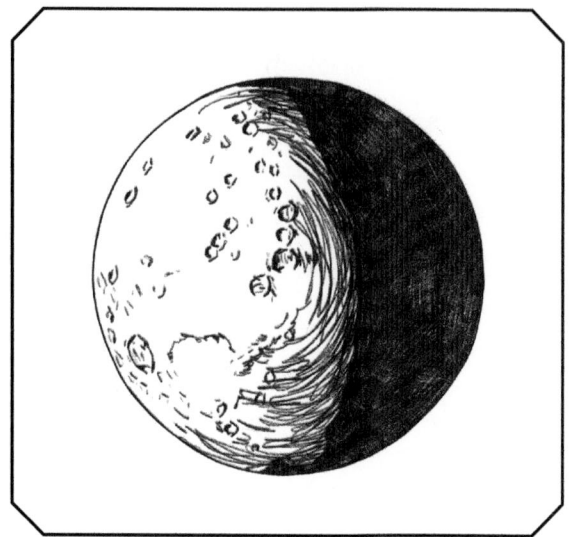

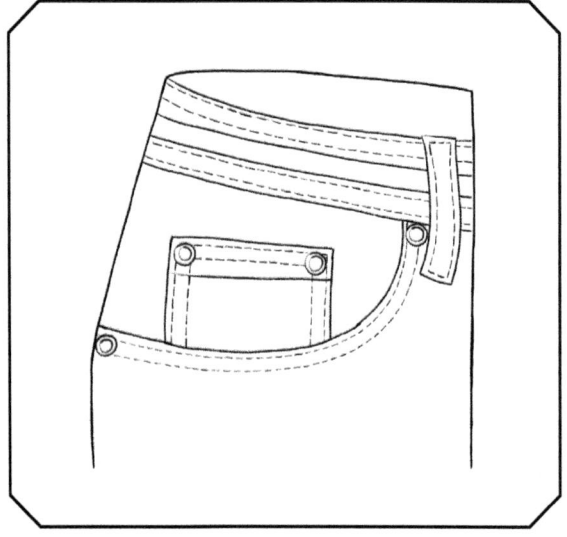

RHYMING PICTURES

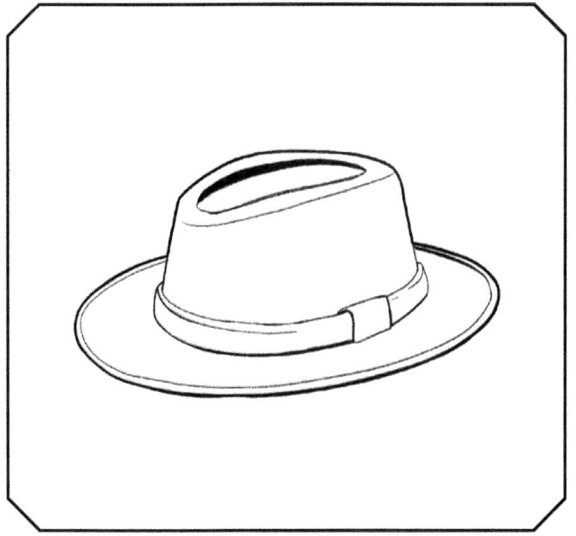

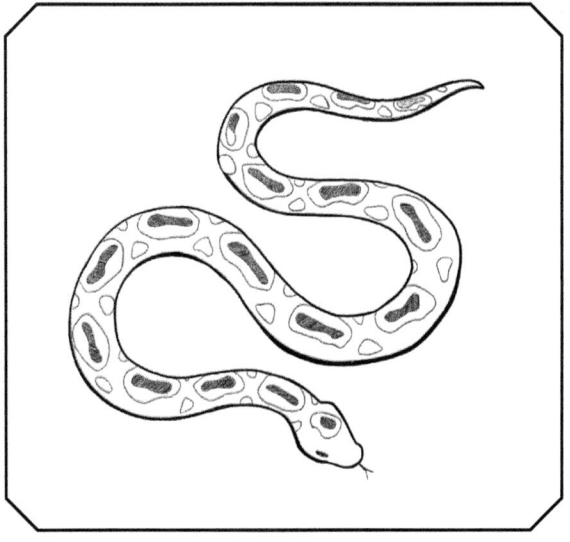
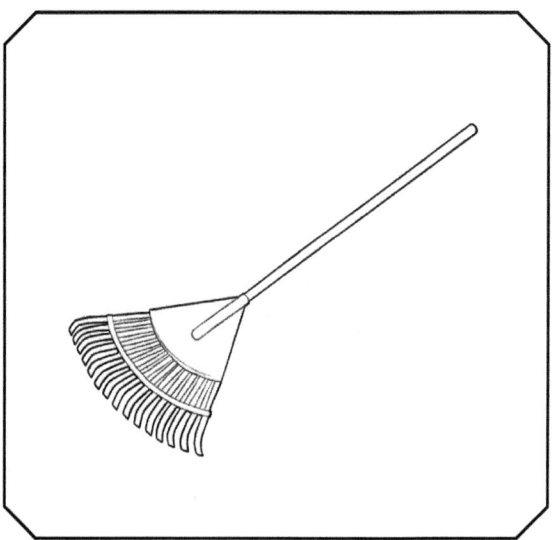

RESOURCE 4

RHYMING PICTURES

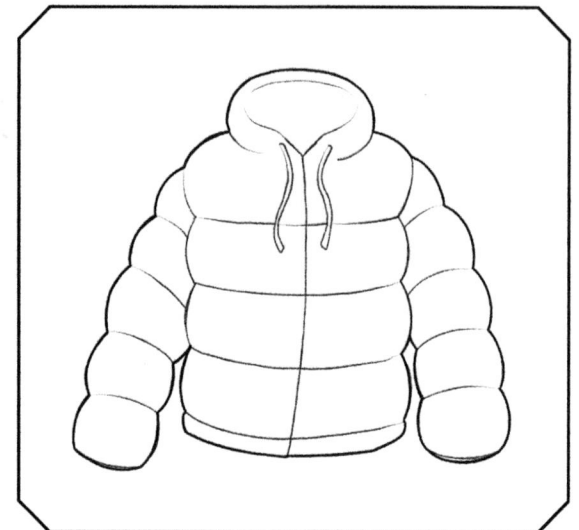

© Bloomsbury Education, 2026

RHYMING PICTURES

RHYMING PICTURES

 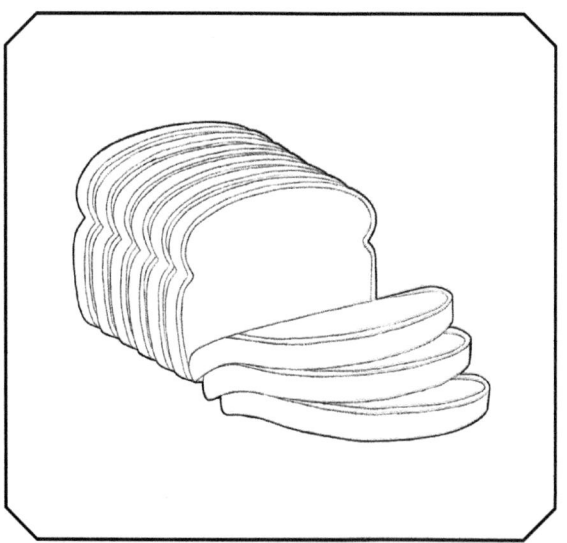

RHYMING PICTURES

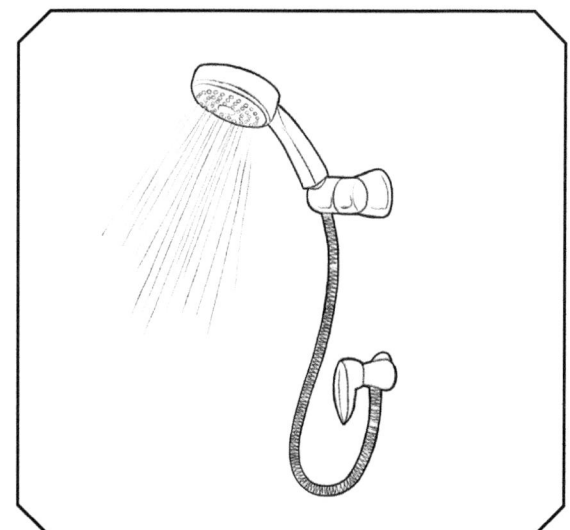

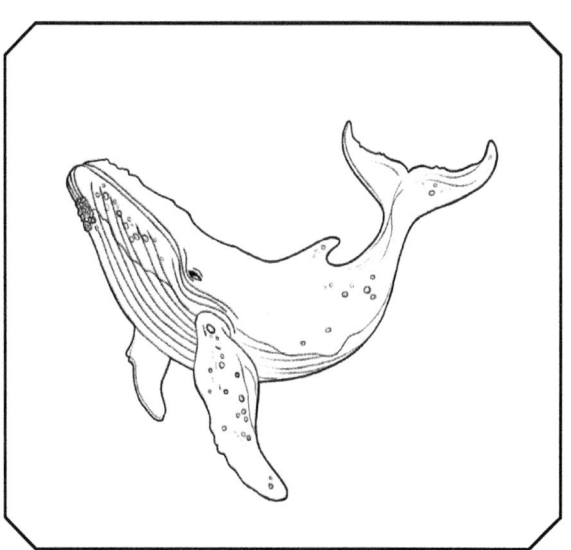
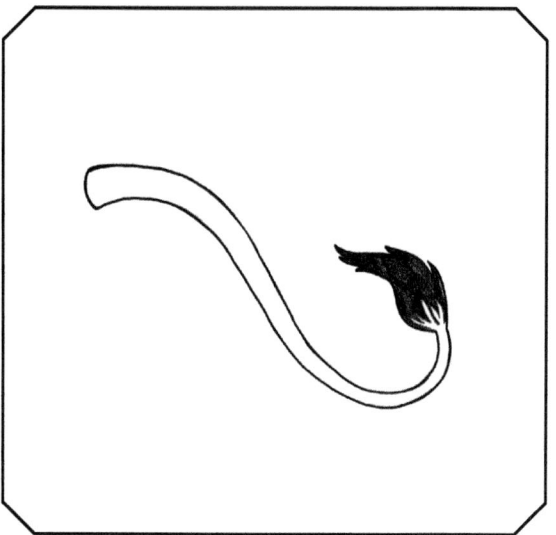

RHYMING PICTURES

Rhyming pairs

sun/bun

shoe/two

clock/sock

spoon/moon

carrot/parrot

pocket/rocket

Rhyming sets

cat/bat/hat

cake/snake/rake

boat/coat/goat

key/tea/sea

car/star/jar

train/plane/rain

chair/pear/bear or hair

bed/shed/head

flower/shower/tower

snail/whale/tail

RESOURCE 5

SEQUENCING CATERPILLAR CARDS

SEQUENCING CATERPILLAR CARDS

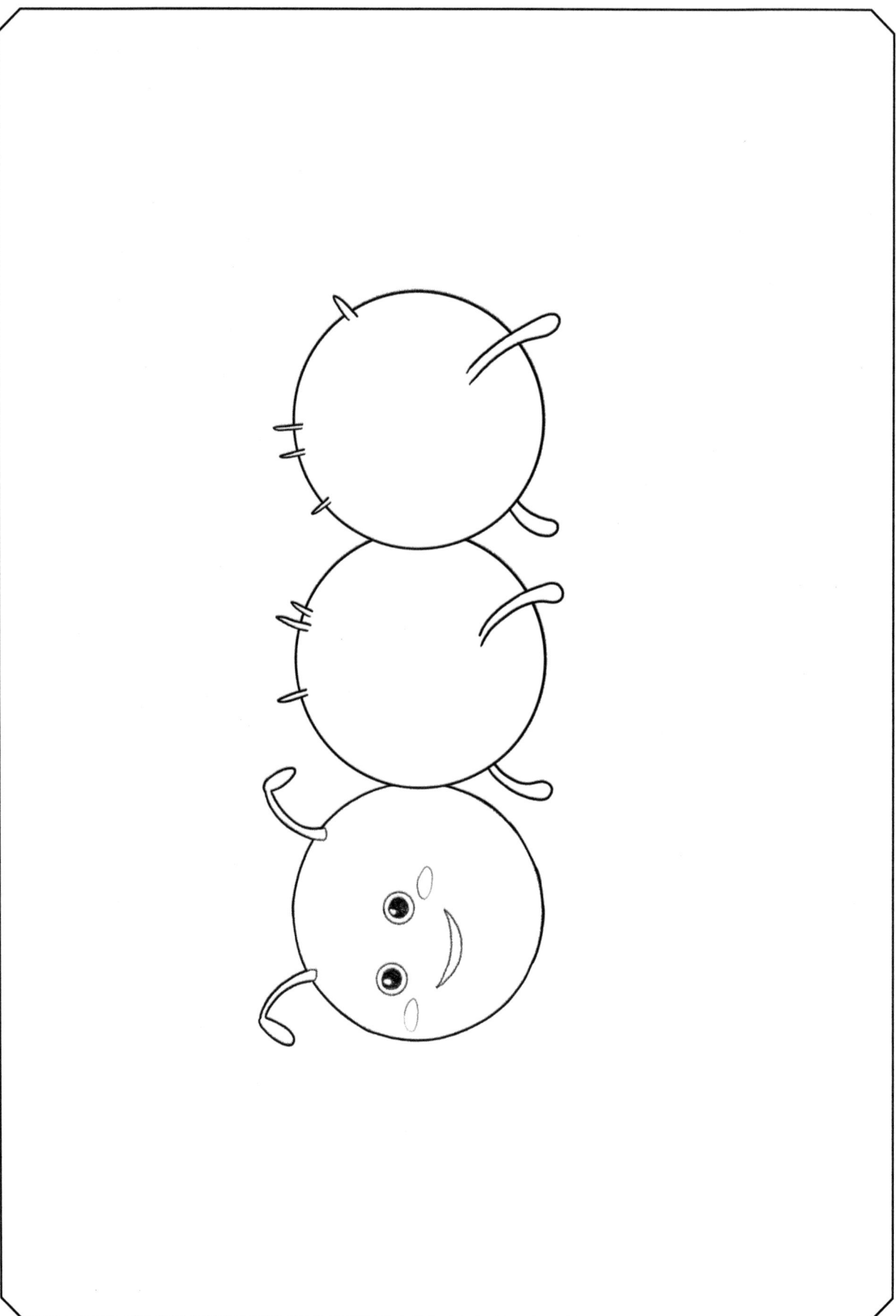

SEQUENCING CATERPILLAR CARDS

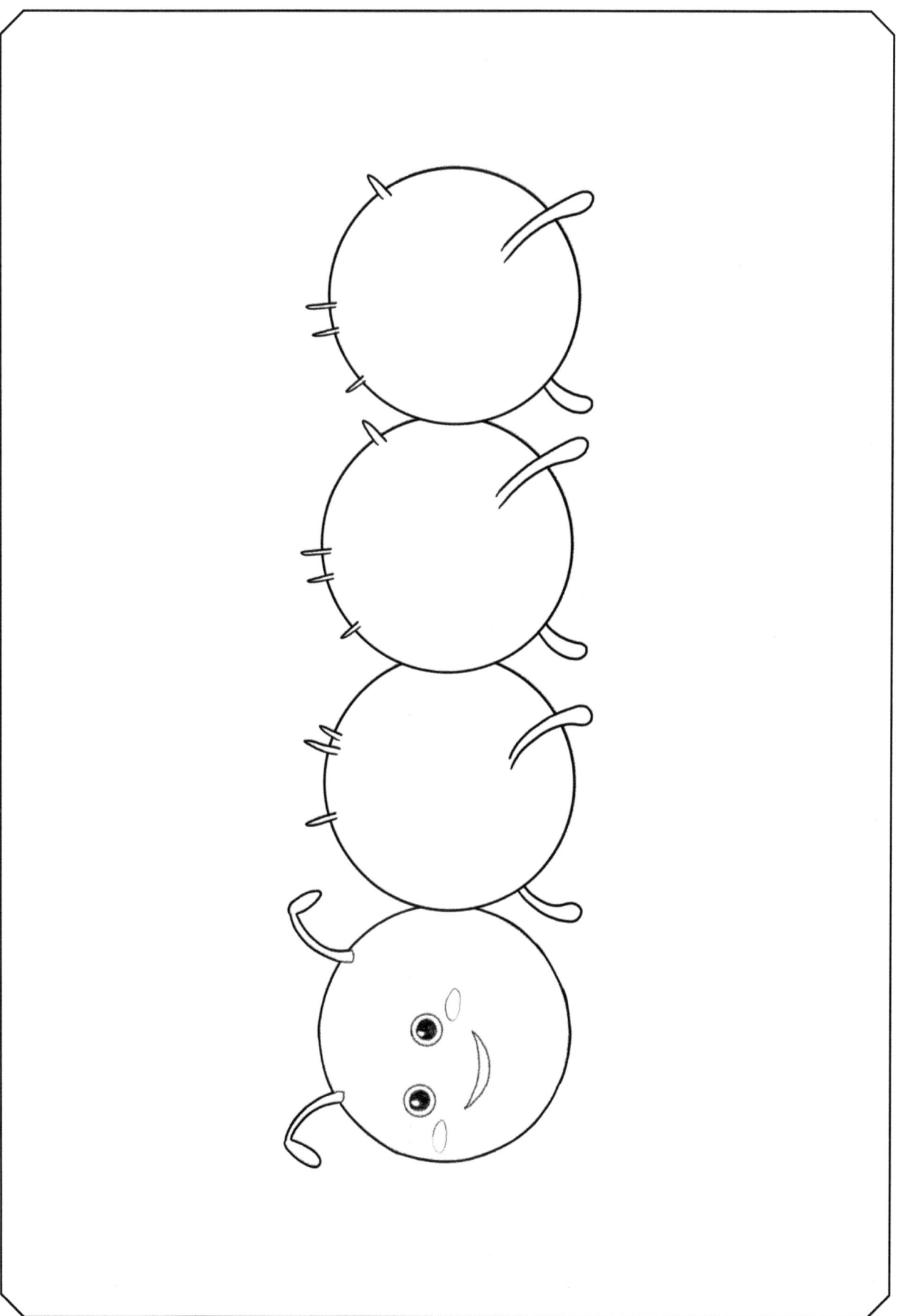

PICNIC RHYMING GAME

Apple:
papple; dapple…babble…gapple…I think we will take a juicy…

Coffee:
loffee; moffee; hoffee; toffee…shall we take a cup of…

Donut:
monut; bonut; sonut; jonut…shall we take a jammy…

Yoghurt:
loghurt; soghurt; roghurt; foghurt…shall we take a pot of…

Crisps:
bisps; wisps; lisps; trisps…shall we take a packet of…

Sandwich:
landwich; bandwich; grandwich; handwich…shall we take a yummy…

Banana:
tanana; panana; fanana; ganana shall we take a ripe…

Jelly:
felly; welly; selly; belly…shall we take a wobbly…

Biscuit:
tiscuit; fiscuit; miscuit; liscuit…shall we take a chocolate…

Water:
sorter; dorter; lorter; morter…shall we take a bottle of water…

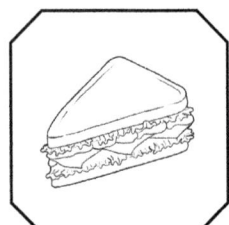 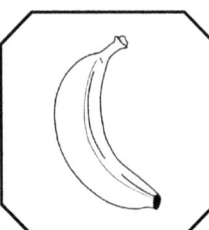  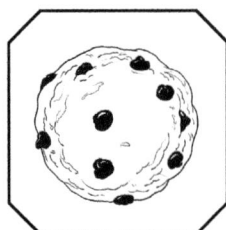 

SYLLABLE PICTURE CARDS (TRANSPORT)

RESOURCE 7

SYLLABLE PICTURE CARDS (MINIBEASTS)

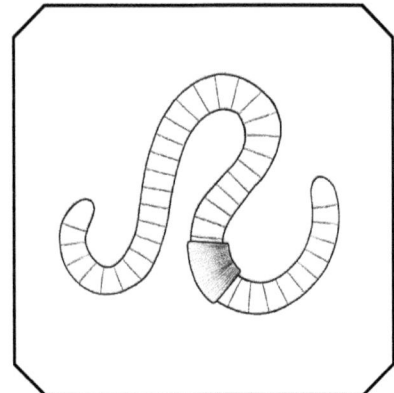
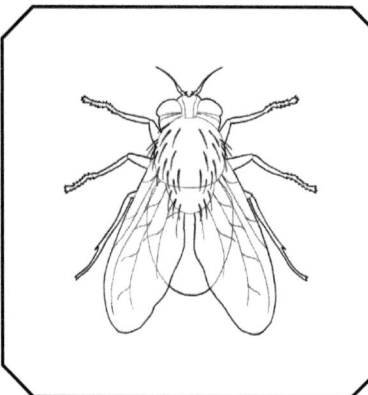
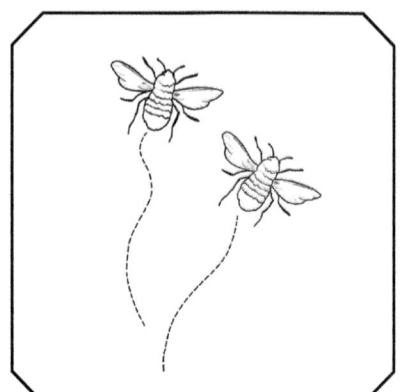

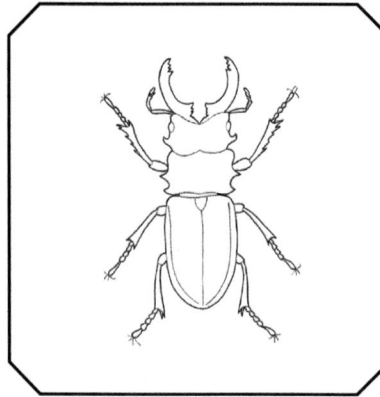
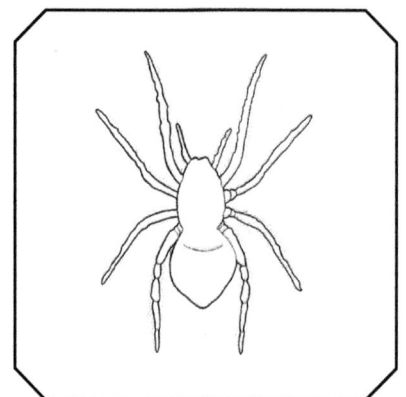

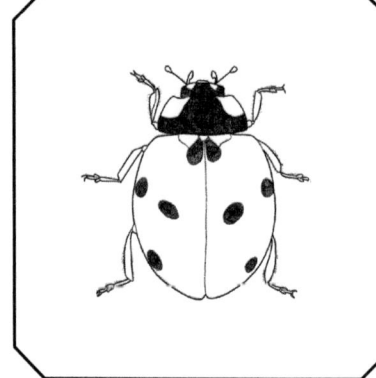

© Bloomsbury Education, 2026

SYLLABLE PICTURE CARDS (FOOD)

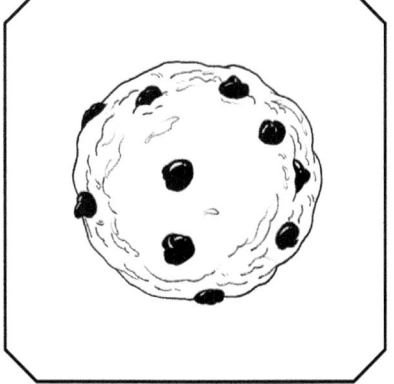
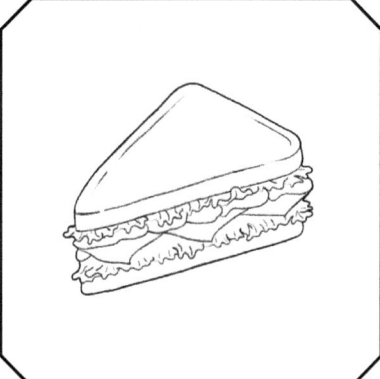

SYLLABLE PICTURE CARDS (ANIMALS)

© Bloomsbury Education, 2026

VOWEL CARDS

 oo

 eye

 ee

RESOURCE 9

ANIMAL PICNIC GAME CARDS

Harry Horse

Lots of mice

Buzzy Bees

Bobby Bear

Larry Lamb

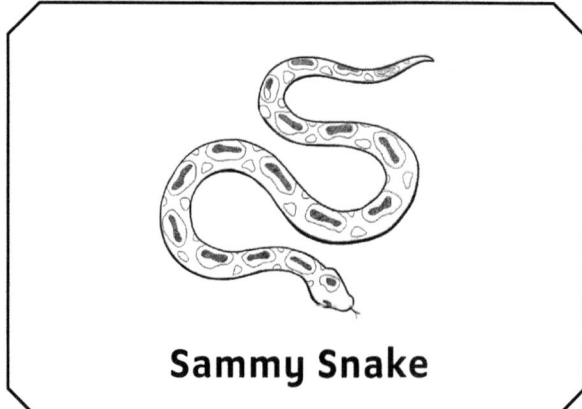
Sammy Snake

Polly Parrot

Gordon Goose

© Bloomsbury Education, 2026

ANIMAL PICNIC GAME CARDS

Picnic foods: sauce/rice/cheese/pear/ham/cake/carrot/juice

RESOURCE 10

COMPOUND WORD PICTURE CARDS

Set 1 – Possible words: Snowman, snowball, postman, postbox, fruitcake, pancake
butterfly, dragonfly, fireman, firefly, shoebox, horseshoe

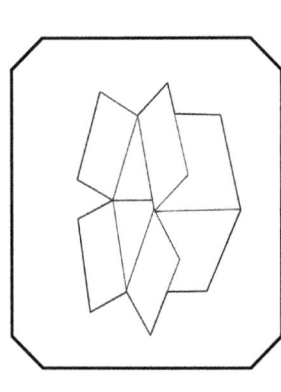

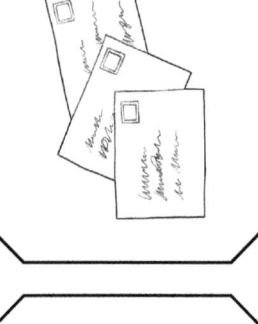
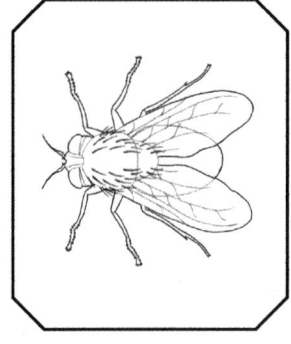

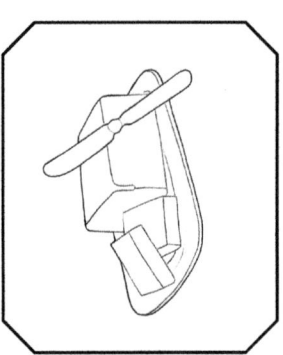

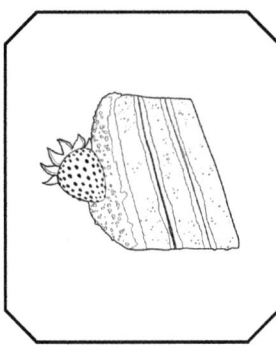

© Bloomsbury Education, 2026

COMPOUND WORD PICTURE CARDS

Set 2 – Possible words:

fishfinger starfish sunflower flowerbed sunbed fishfood birdfood
lighthouse ladybird birdhouse carpark carwash sunlight starlight

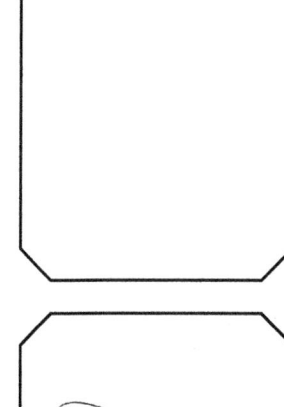
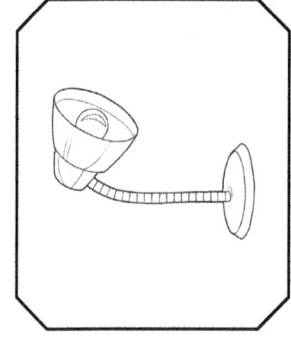

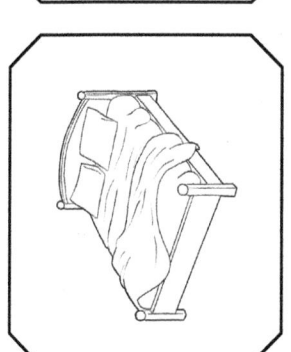

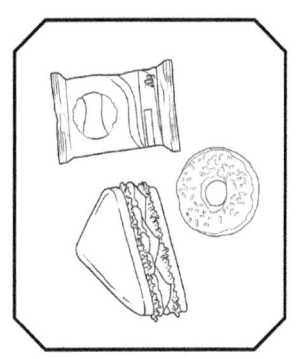
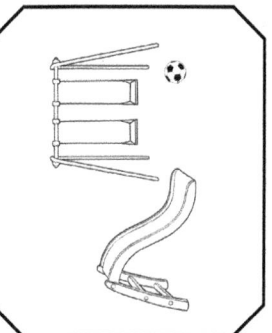

RESOURCE 11

SYLLABLE-BLENDING PICTURE CARDS

Syllable blending words:

lemon/letter   pencil/penguin   circus/circle   money/monkey

lolly/lorry   button/butter   rattle/rabbit

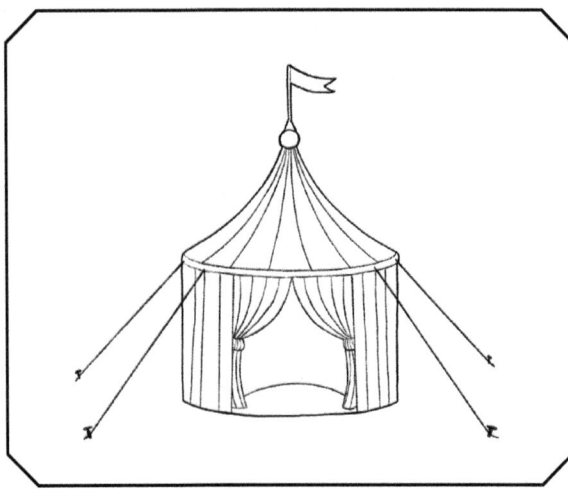
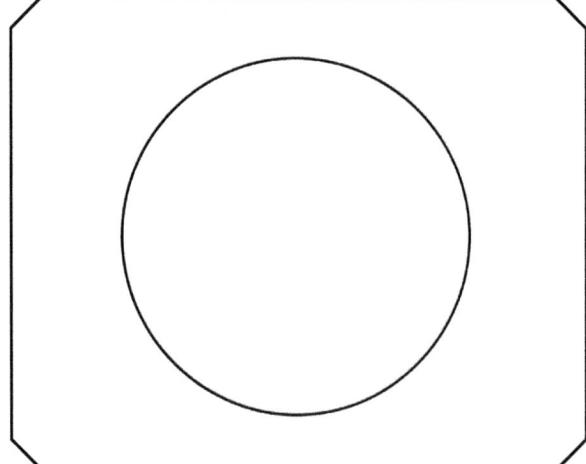

© Bloomsbury Education, 2026

SYLLABLE-BLENDING PICTURE CARDS

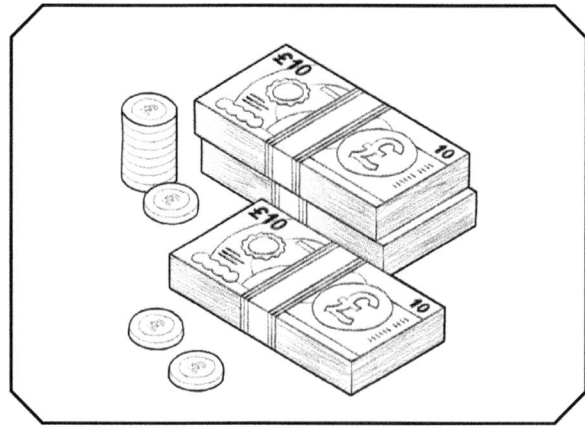

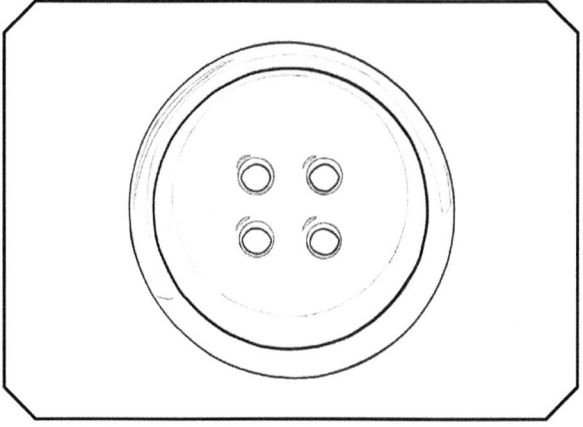
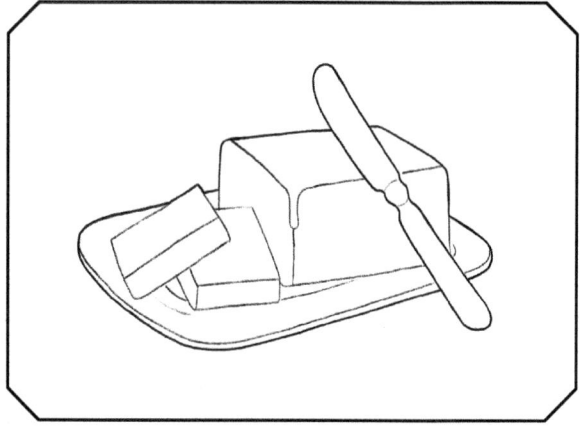
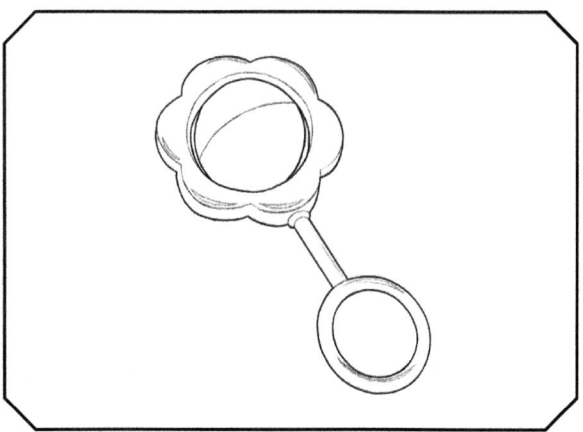

YES/NO CARDS

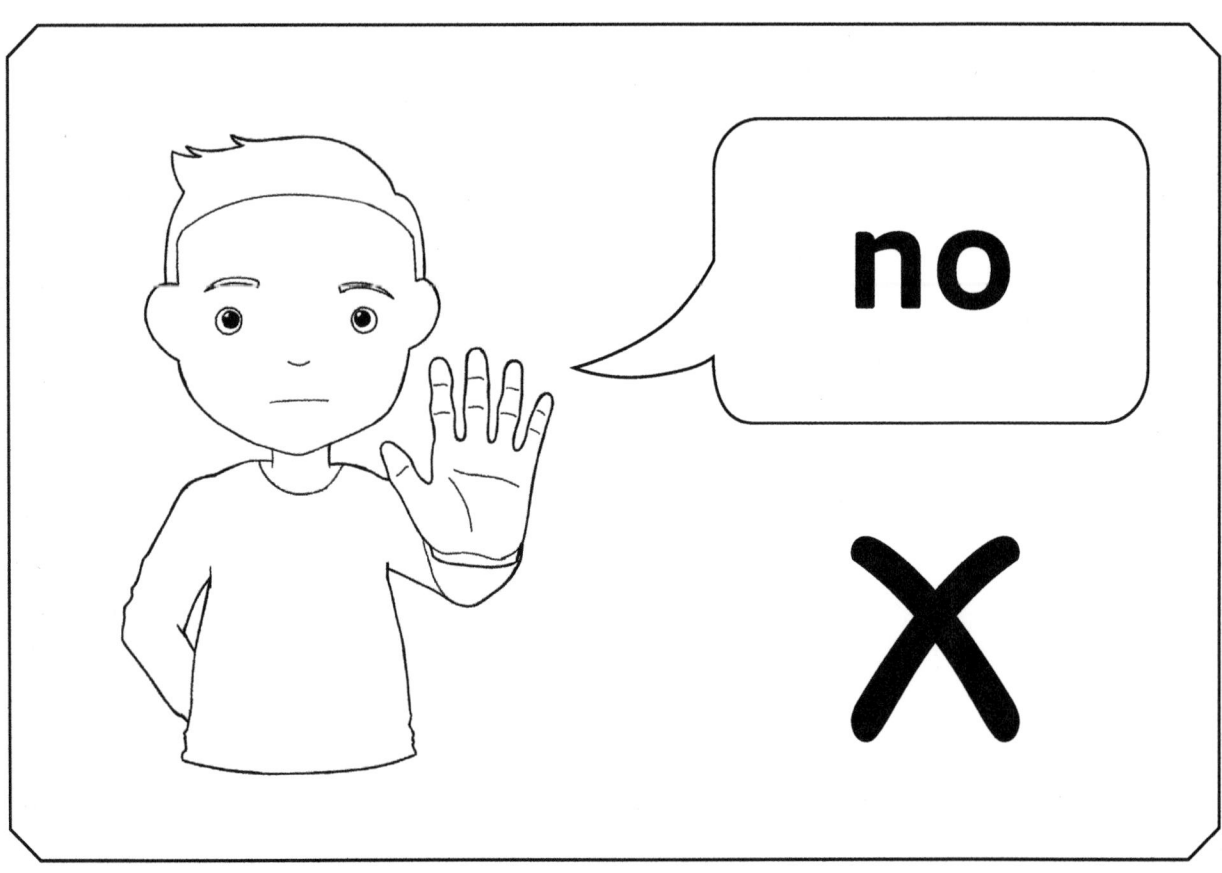

RESOURCE 13

VC WORD LISTS

Step down VC words	VC words	Step up VC words
am/is	it/if	an/am
if/at	an/at	if/is
an/it	am/as	in/an
in/as	is/in	as/is

© Bloomsbury Education, 2026

RESOURCE 14

INITIAL SOUND PICTURES

© Bloomsbury Education, 2026

INITIAL SOUND PICTURES

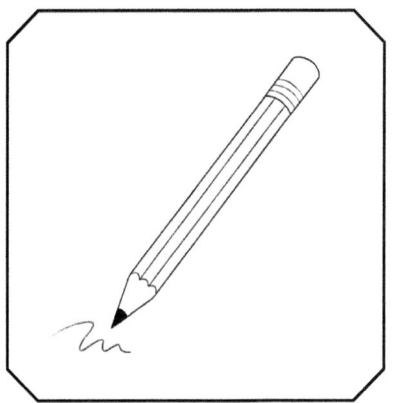

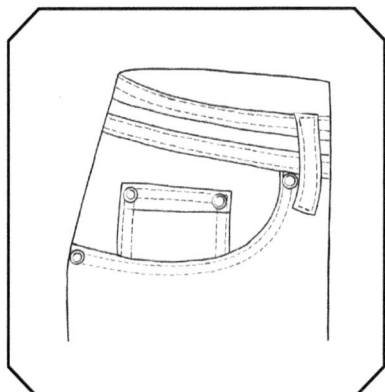

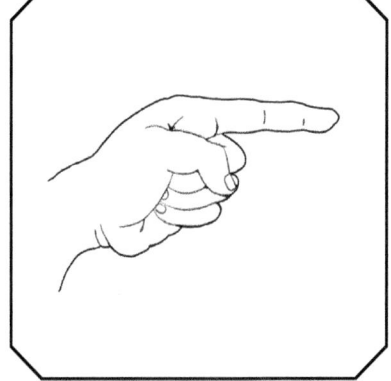

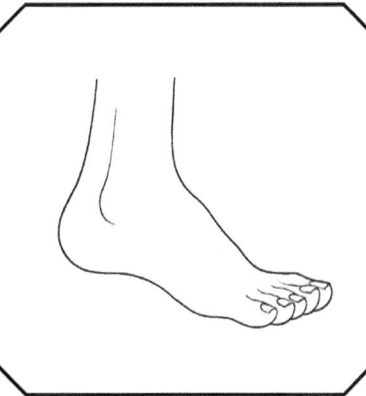

INITIAL SOUND PICTURES

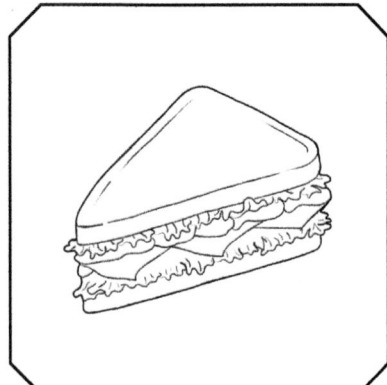

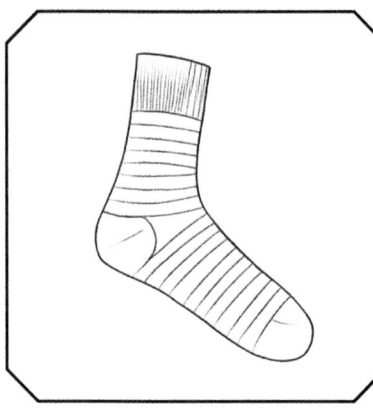

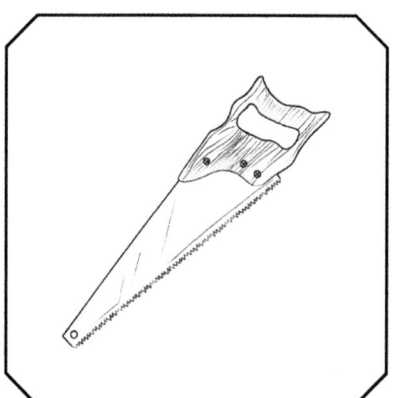

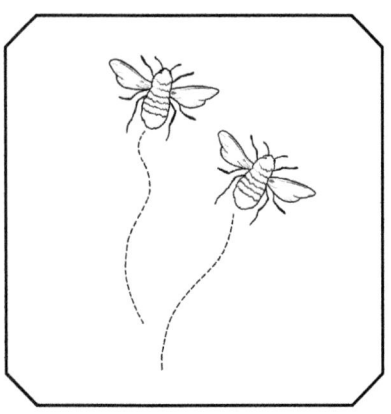

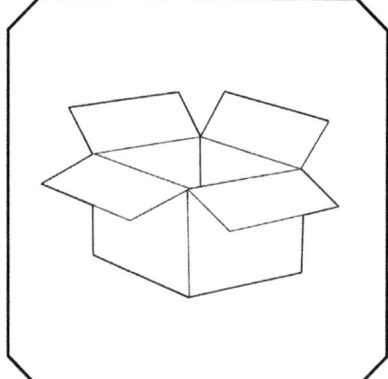

INITIAL SOUND PICTURES

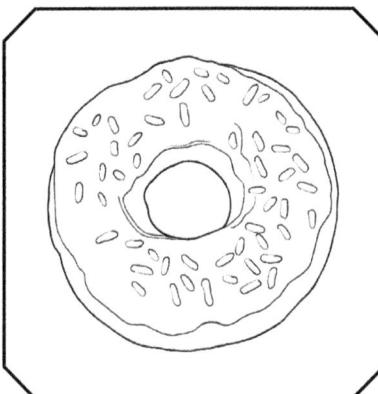

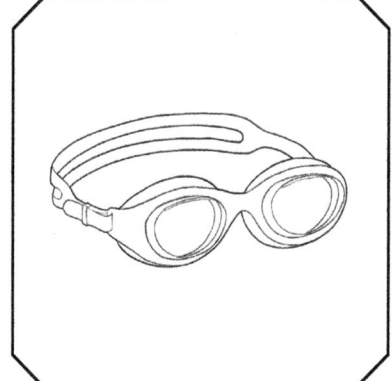

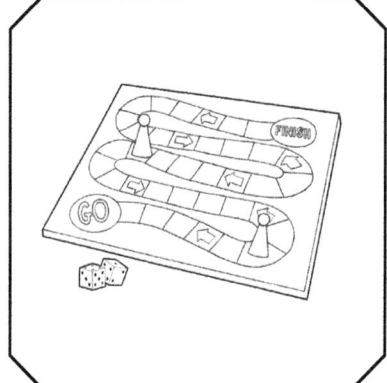

INITIAL SOUND PICTURES

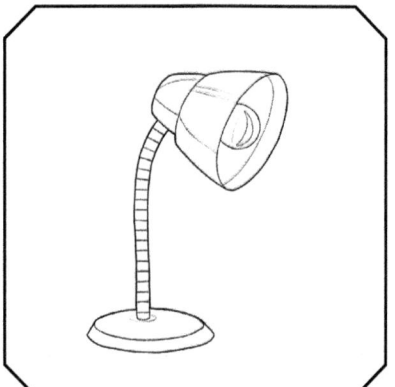
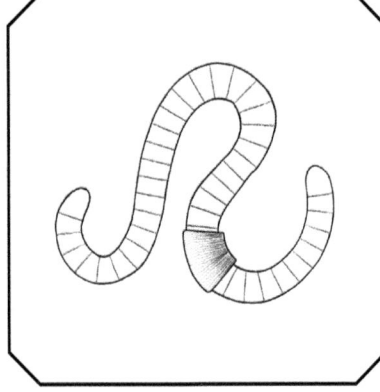

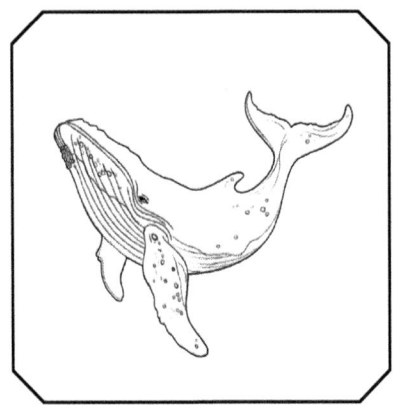
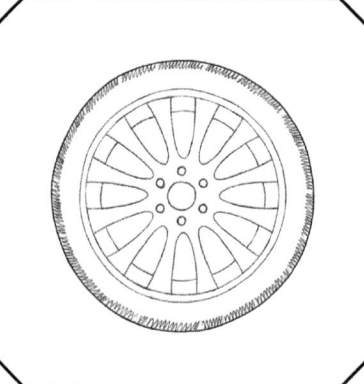
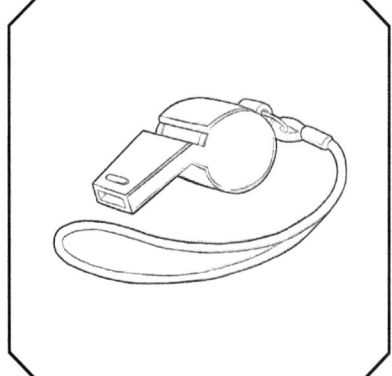

INITIAL SOUND PICTURES

Word List:

/l/	/w/
lolly	worm
ladder	watch
lamb	water
leaf	whale
lemon	wheel
light	whistle

/d/	/g/
duck	ghost
dice	goat
dog	goggles
dolphin	goose
donut	girl
door	game

/s/	/b/
sandwich	bag
sea	bear
six	bed
sock	bees
sun	boat
saw	box

/p/	/f/
pan	fire
pear	fish
pencil	finger
penguin	five
pig	foot
pocket	four

/k/	/t/
car	two
cake	tea
cow	tent
cat	tie
key	table
carrot	tower

RESOURCE 15

MINIMAL PAIR PICTURES

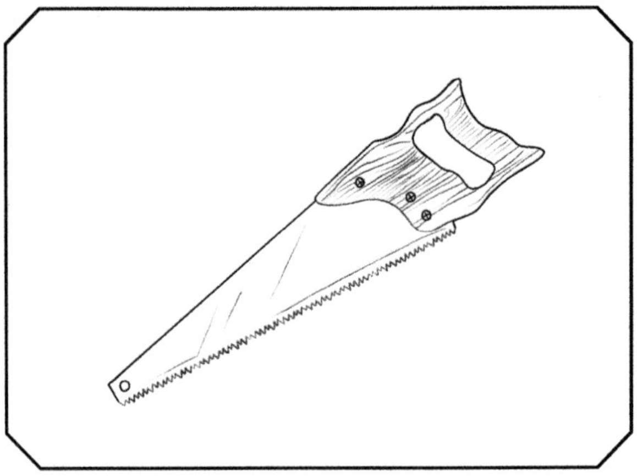

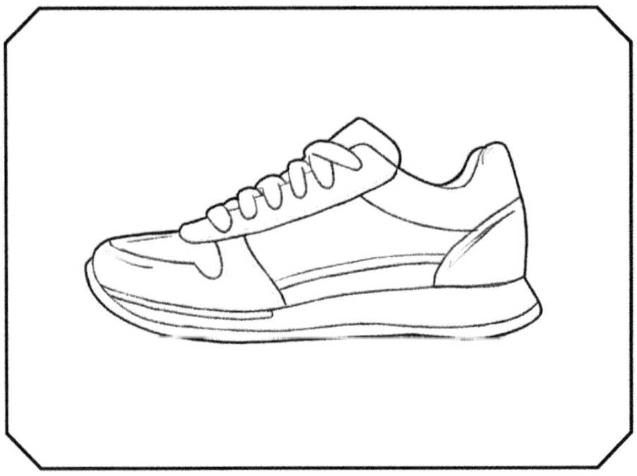

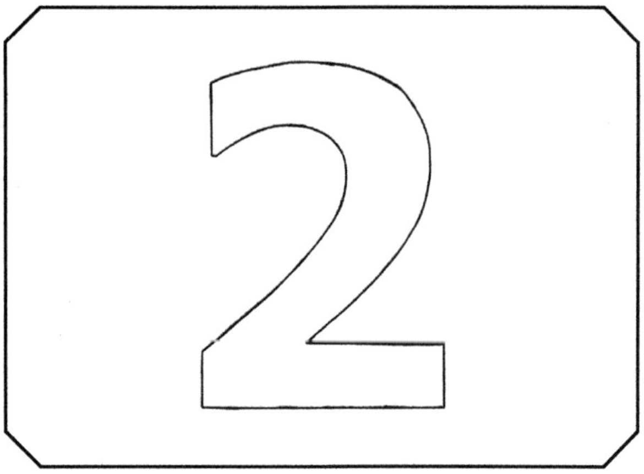

MINIMAL PAIR PICTURES

Pear/bear   saw/door   shoe/two   tea/key
white/light   tick/kick   fair/bear   four/door

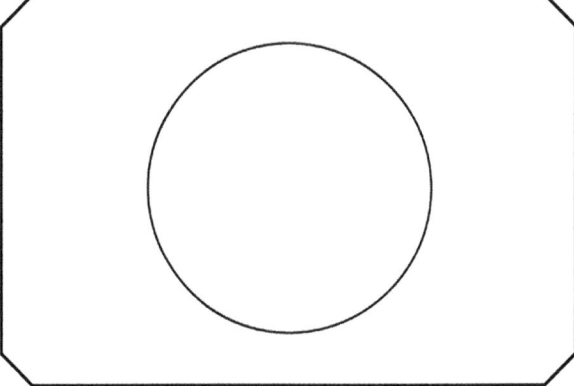
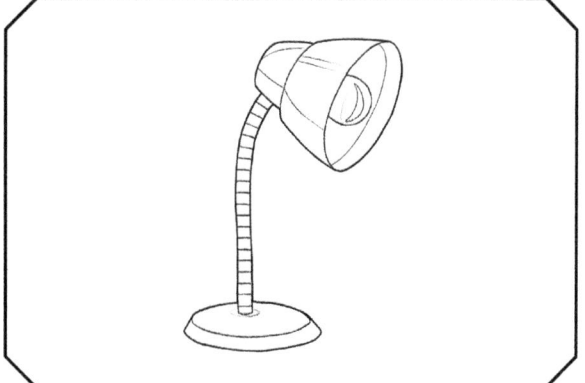
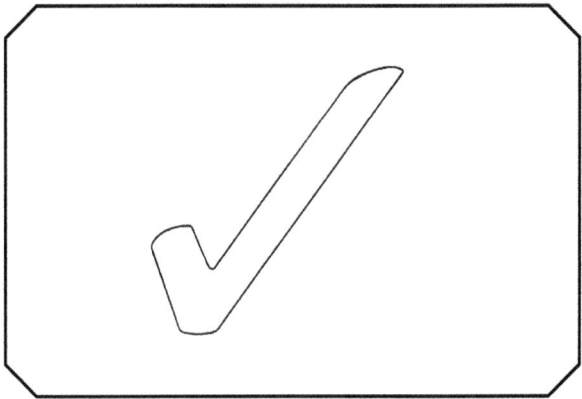

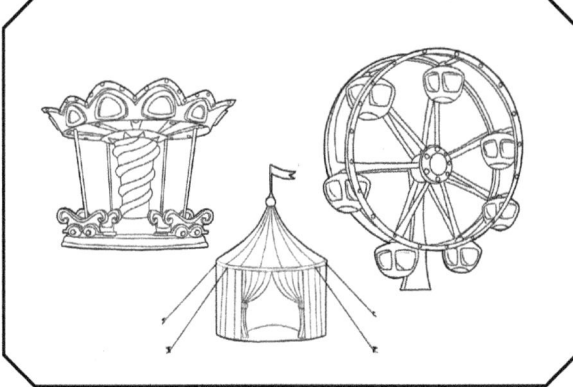

RESOURCE 16

WORD TAKEAWAY LISTS

Suffix: careless, walking, cheerful, quickly, painful, harmless, loudly, climbing, helpless, eating, colourful, sadly

Prefix: unhappy, disagree, mistrust, reread, discount, misheard, undo, regain, dismiss, misplace, recount, unclear

First sound: mice, cold, ditch, gate, cup, pin, sand, beach, hill, cake, feet, boat, price, plate, stand, snake, treat, float

Syllable: monkey, carpet, candle, beetle, spider, station, robot, honey, careful, harvest, table, rabbit

Compound word: firework, skateboard, ice cream, rainbow, sandwich, football, bedroom, microwave, playground, lunchbox, lightbulb, seahorse

RHYME JUDGEMENT PICTURES

Do they rhyme or not? (week 10 and week 20)

 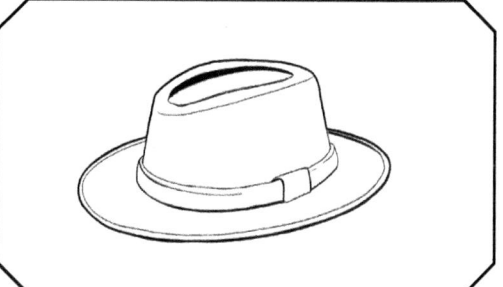

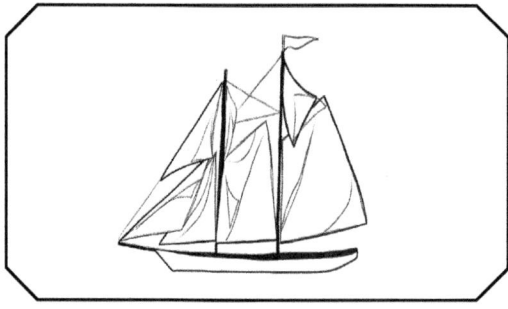 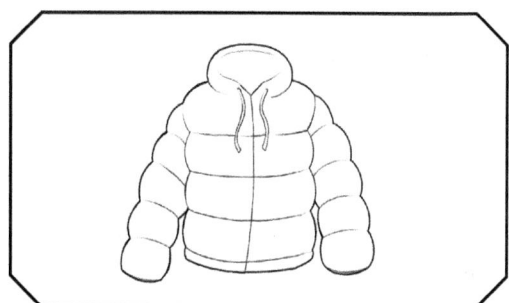

© Bloomsbury Education, 2026

RHYME JUDGEMENT PICTURES

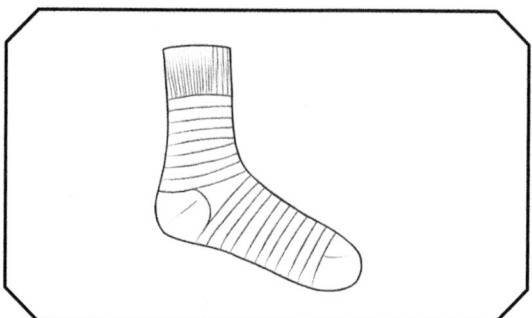
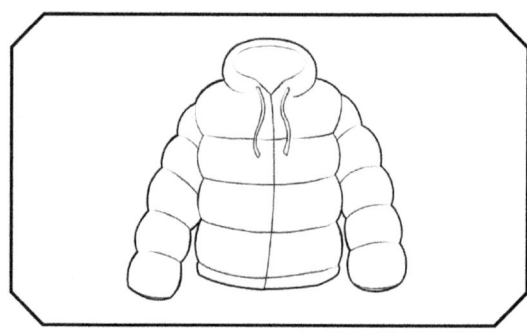

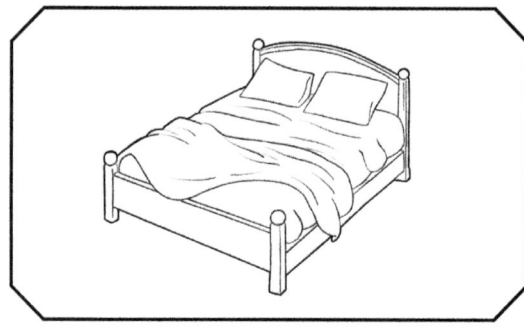

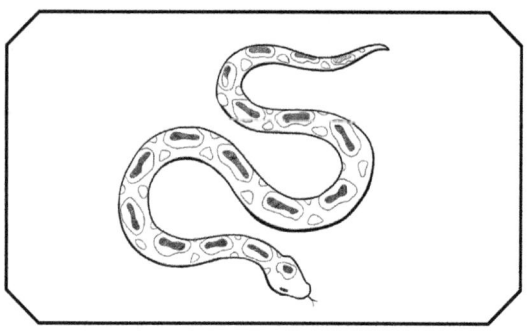

RHYME JUDGEMENT PICTURES

Odd one out (week 12 and week 22)

RESOURCE 17

RHYME JUDGEMENT PICTURES

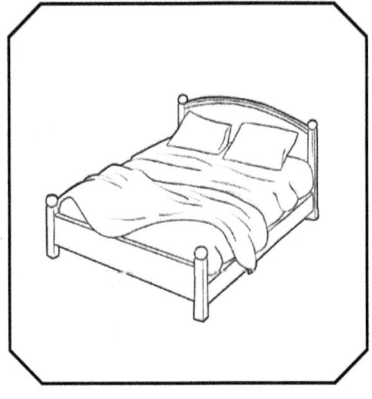

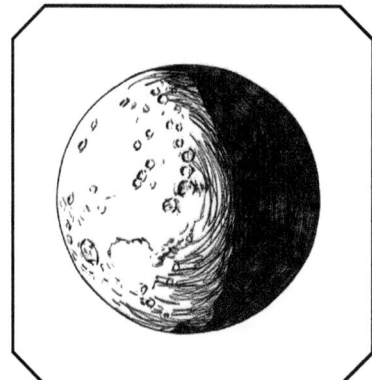

© Bloomsbury Education, 2026

RESOURCE 18

FINAL SOUND PICTURES

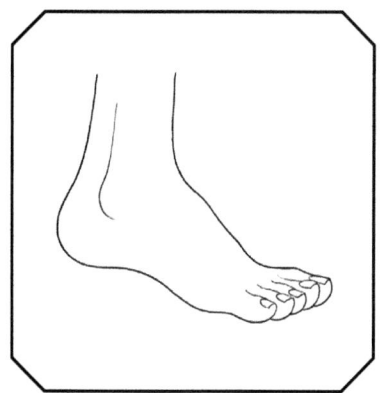

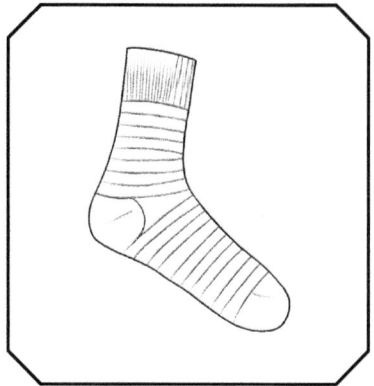

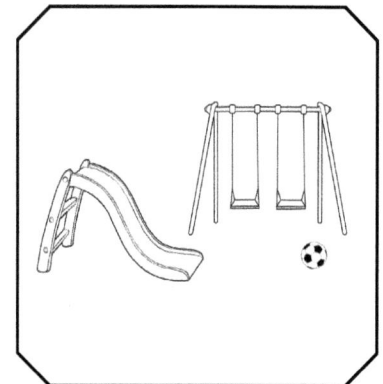

© Bloomsbury Education, 2026

RESOURCE 18

FINAL SOUND PICTURES

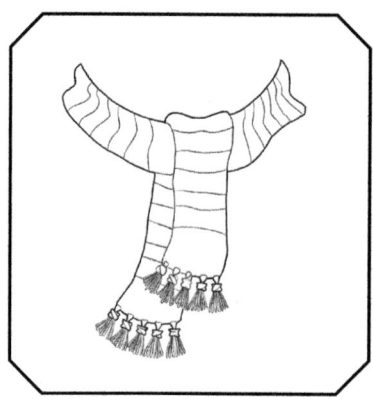

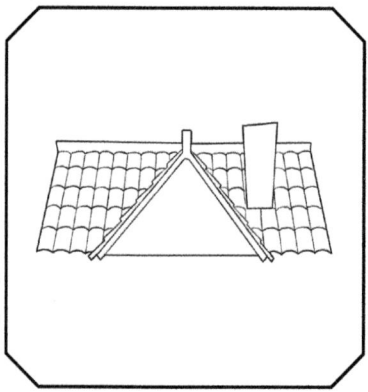
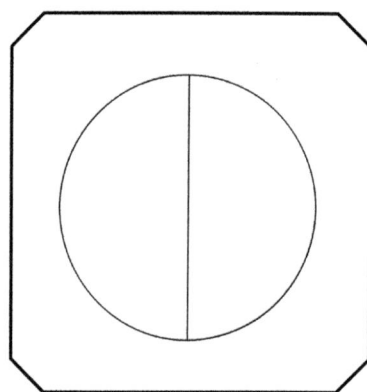

© Bloomsbury Education, 2026

FINAL SOUND PICTURES

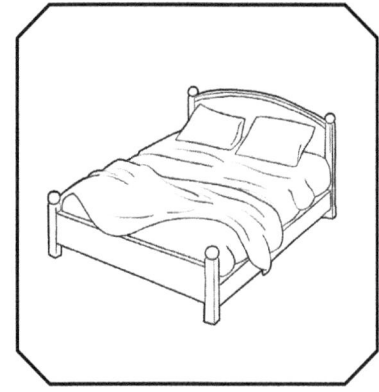  

  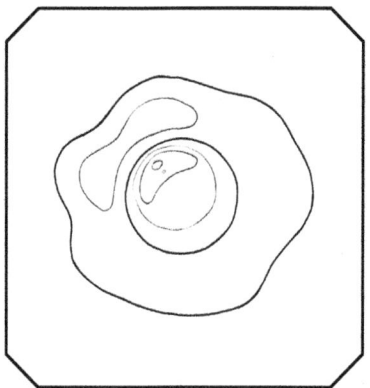

  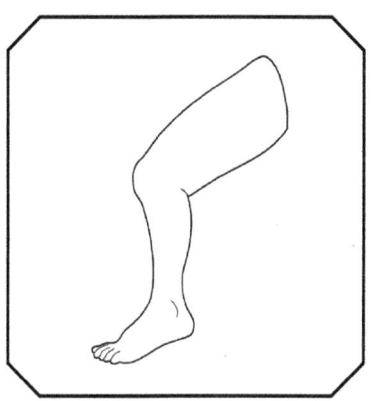

FINAL SOUND PICTURES

Word List:

/-t/	/-f/	/-d/
cat	leaf	bed
foot	scarf	sword
light	knife	shed
sweet	roof	food
hat	half	road
carrot	laugh	bird

/-k/	/-s/	/-g/
sock	dice	dog
cake	goose	bag
duck	horse	egg
snake	juice	frog
park	sauce	pig
bike	house	leg

WORD CHAIN LISTS

Compound word	Syllable	First sound	
firework	monkey	mice	feet
skateboard	carpet	cold	boat
ice cream	candle	ditch	price
rainbow	beetle	gate	plate
sandwich	spider	cup	stand
football	station	pin	snake
bedroom	robot	sand	treat
microwave	honey	beach	float
playground	careful	hill	
lunchbox	harvest	cake	
lightbulb	table		
seahorse	rabbit		

Prefix	Suffix
unhappy	careless
disagree	walking
mistrust	cheerful
reread	quickly
discount	painful
misheard	harmless
undo	loudly
regain	climbing
dismiss	helpless
misplace	eating
recount	colourful
unclear	sadly

WIN THE RHYME WORD LISTS

Easier:			Trickier:						
Rhyming picture:	Letters		Rhyming picture:	Letters					
key	b	s	cat	h	s	b	m	f	p
car	f	b	chair	h	p	b	f	t	c
shoe	t	d	sun	b	f	g	r	w	t
shower	t	p	cake	r	b	t	l	m	f
rocket	s	l	bed	r	h	s	f	l	d
whale	t	n	cow	n	r	b	p	w	n

© Bloomsbury Education, 2026

SAME/DIFFERENT CUE CARD

different

same

SAME/DIFFERENT JUDGEMENT WORD LISTS

first sound; real	first sound; nonsense	last sound; real	last sound; nonsense	middle sound; real	middle sound; nonsense
bin/tin	biv/tiv	web/well	wab/wal	pen/pan	ped/pid
map/map	mal/mal	can/can	cag/cag	not/nut	nol/nul
net/pet	nep/kep	pin/pig	pib/pid	bed/bed	bep/bep
mug/jug	mul/jul	hot/hop	hod/hol	sick/sack	zick/zack
top/top	tob/tob	mud/mug	muv/mub	map/map	mel/mel
jam/lamb	taz/laz	get/get	gell/gell	rod/red	rog/reg
cot/dot	con/don	back/bad	baf/bam	hut/hot	hup/hap
fan/fan	zid/did	sit/sit	sif/sif	bag/beg	bal/bul
zip/tip	wep/wep	log/lot	lod/lon	kiss/kiss	tiss/tiss
web/web	tol/col	fuss/fuss	fup/fup	log/leg	lan/lin
cap/tap	caf/taf	mad/mat	mal/mab	tin/ten	tiv/tev
not/not	nos/nos	bed/beg	bef/bech	mud/mad	mub/mab
hut/nut	ket/tet	sick/sit	tol/tol	lot/lot	loz/loz
gun/gun	gub/gub	lock/lock	san/san	sit/sat	sij/saj
lid/did	lis/dis	sum/sum	nup/nup	dug/dig	dup/dep
pen/ten	peb/teb	man/map	ped/pel	pad/pad	pag/pag
bell/tell	bal/fal	run/run	rus/ruv	bad/bed	beck/bick
bag/bag	dag/dag	can/cap	kif/kij	fun/fin	fub/feb
tick/sick	teck/seck	lid/lip	luss/luss	dip/dip	mid/mid
dog/log	sup/dup	red/red	jeg/jek	cup/cap	kun/ken

Step down

middle sound: long vowels (real words)		middle sound: long vowels (nonsense words)	
bean/barn	pipe/peep	feep/foop	soob/soob
hoop/hoop	night/night	harg/harg	nide/nood
cart/kite	seat/suit	pide/pard	bime/bime
heat/heart	food/feed	charg/choog	jook/jike
farm/farm	bead/bead	dipe/darp	reen/rarn
sheet/shoot	mine/mean	keeb/kibe	koom/kime
read/ride	sharp/sheep	jine/jarn	nart/nart
cheat/chart	root/right	leeb/leeb	woov/wive
room/rhyme	shark/shark	jart/jight	marb/meeb
bike/beak	choose/cheese	deem/darm	keet/koot

GAME BOARD

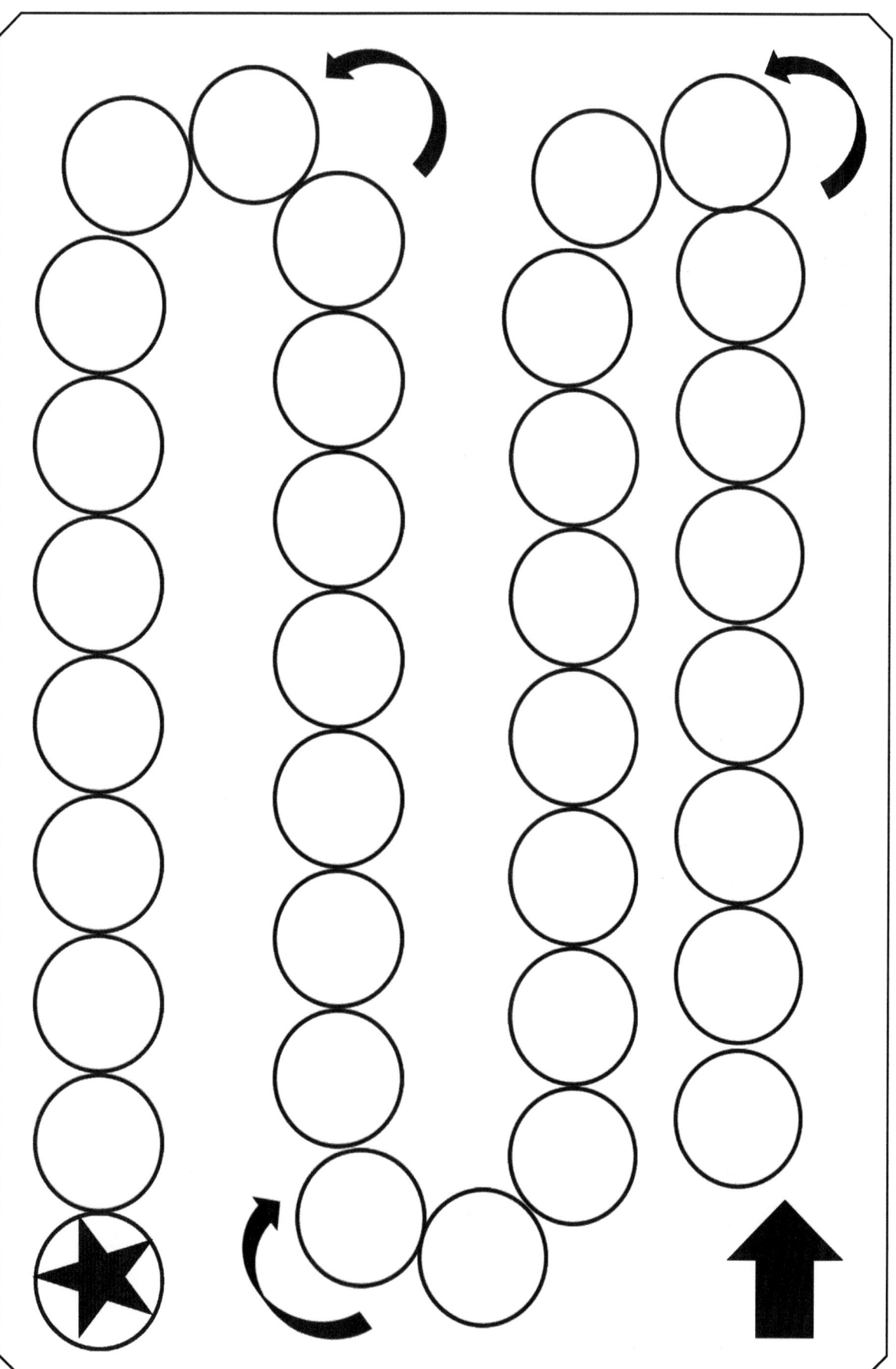

SYLLABLE DOMINOES

SYLLABLE DOMINOES

RESOURCE 24

SYLLABLE DOMINOES

SYLLABLE DOMINOES

RESOURCE 25

IS MY SOUND IN THE WORD?

Real words:

\			Sound in a word?			
b	**f**	**t**	**d**	**k**	**g**	**s**
big	fish	ten	dice	case	ghost	sun
bell	bin	cake	red	rock	frog	soap
fun	foot	bat	cot	kite	gap	kiss
web	sock	lock	date	tape	comb	tail
pin	loaf	teeth	log	coat	sack	dig
rub	farm	tick	mud	sock	big	mess
leaf	ball	duck	goal	leg	get	not
bag	face	sit	dot	cough	call	seat
top	half	mad	bag	back	dip	bus
robe	fall	light	sad	goose	bad	fat

Nonsense words:

			Sound in a word?			
b	**f**	**t**	**d**	**k**	**g**	**s**
bulv	tif	tib	delg	kuz	gach	liss
teb	fape	pite	pog	kiv	dag	sab
bod	beej	tev	duss	pock	gelb	jat
bink	fowk	tonk	lud	kimp	dut	suth
wup	fide	taz	dowb	teb	gim	sog
bep	wob	dak	ket	kag	seck	pess
kif	fal	tulv	dake	tog	gop	sep
balt,	fod	teeb	dorb	keej	wug	tid
baid	luff	zuck	deef	kood	kol	sib
lub	bej	dep	pid	mot	geen	sut

ADD A SYLLABLE STEP UP PICTURES

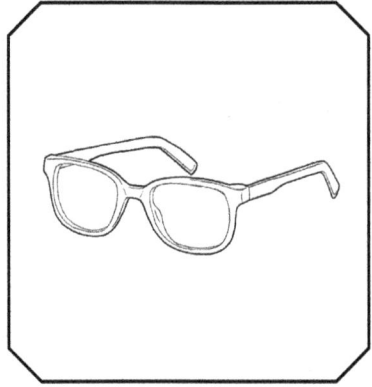  

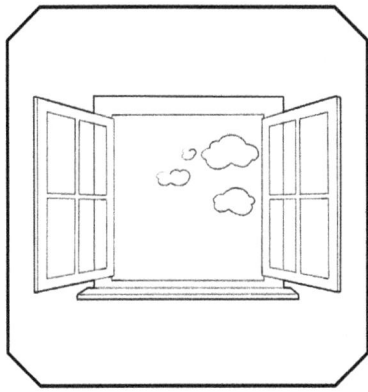  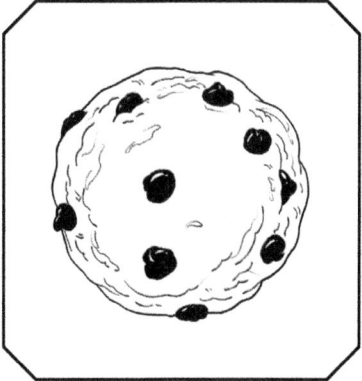

WHERE IN THE WORD?

	t	f	s	d	l	k
Beginning	table	fairy	scissors	doughnut	lemon	carrot
	talking	forest	santa	donkey	ladder	castle
	tiger	feather	singing	digger	lorry	camel
Middle	letter	toffee	listen	middle	jelly	bucket
	water	coughing	messy	reading	balloon	circle
	cutting	puffin	guessing	shadow	falling	chicken
End	robot	giraffe	cactus	horrid	kettle	panic
	rabbit	handcuff	walrus	forehead	puddle	comic
	pirate	relief	nervous	cupboard	football	attic

REAL AND NONSENSE WORDS

Real VC words	Nonsense VC words
am	ap
at	ak
as	af
an	ip
is	ot
if	os
in	om
on	ok
up	uk
us	ut

Real CVC words	Nonsense CVC words
hat	hap
map	cag
bin	tiv
lid	pib
pen	bep
red	reg
lot	lod
dog	rog
cup	ruv
run	fub

© Bloomsbury Education, 2026

FINAL SOUND / NO FINAL SOUND

NO FINAL SOUND

RESOURCE 29

FINAL SOUND

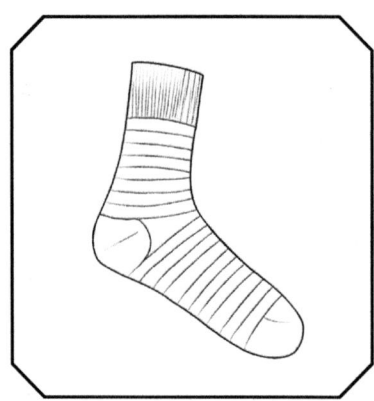

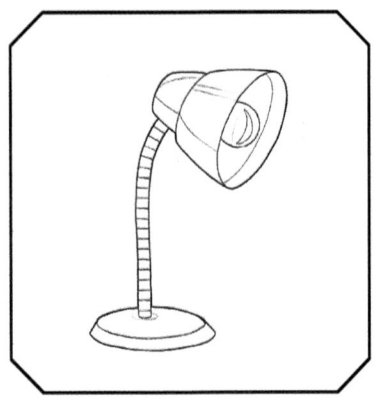
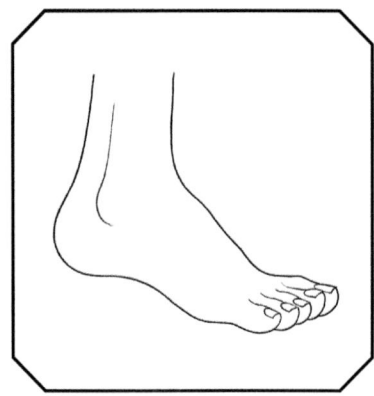

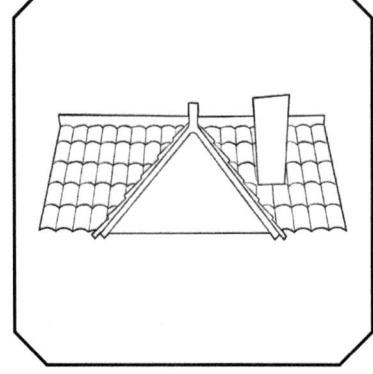

TRICKY SYLLABLE PICTURE CARDS

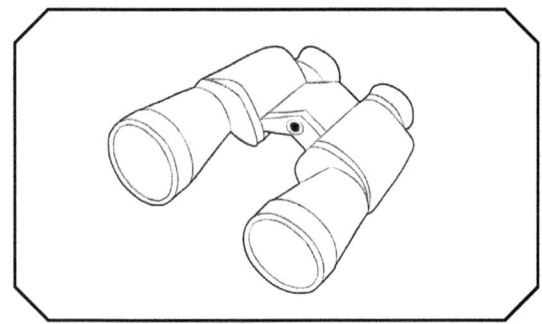

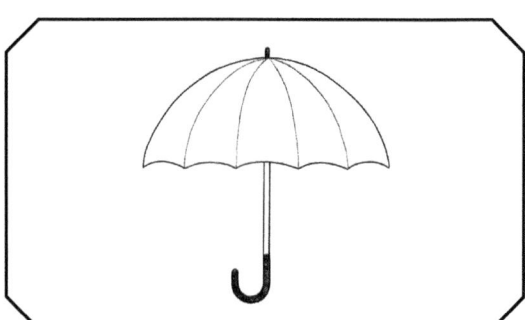

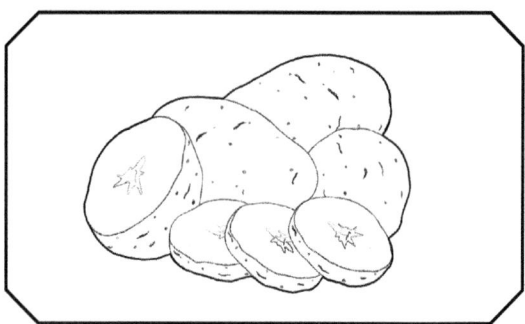

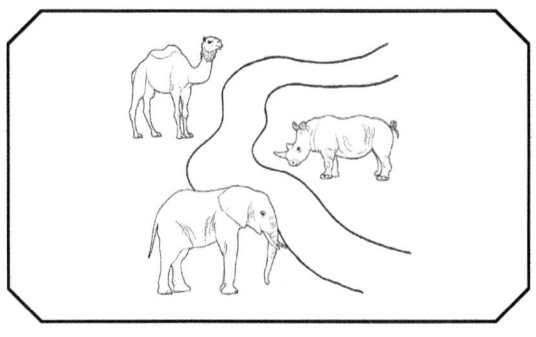

CCVC WORD LISTS

'l' blends	's' blends
clap	slug
flip	stop
flap	snap
slap	slam
clip	skip
slip	swim
flop	step
slop	spot
slot	spin
clot	slip
blot	slam
plot	stun
plug	
slug	
plan	
flan	

ONE AND TWO CARDS

'L' BLEND MINIMAL PAIRS CARDS

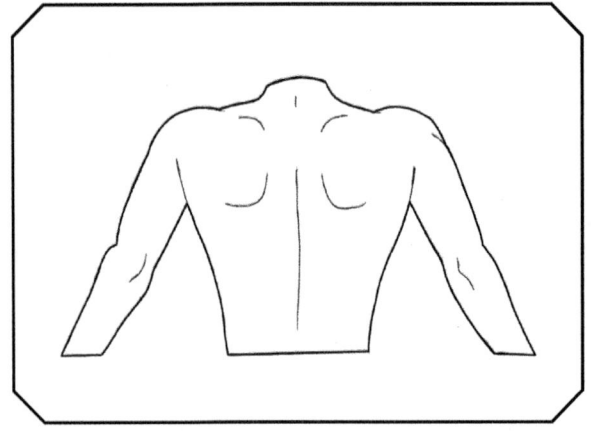

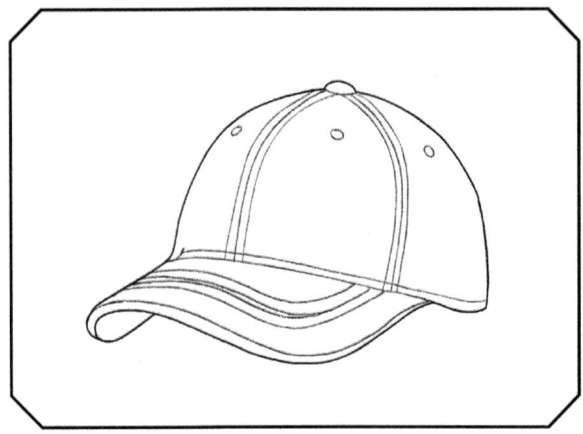
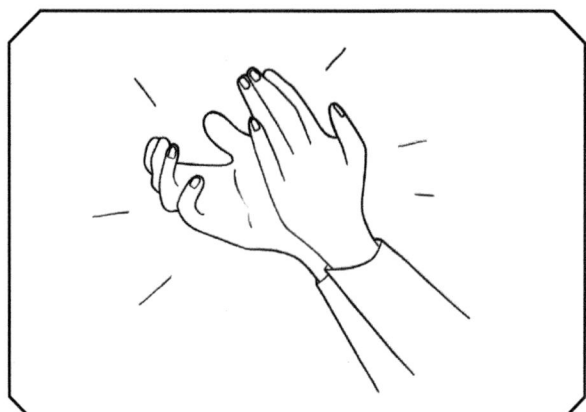
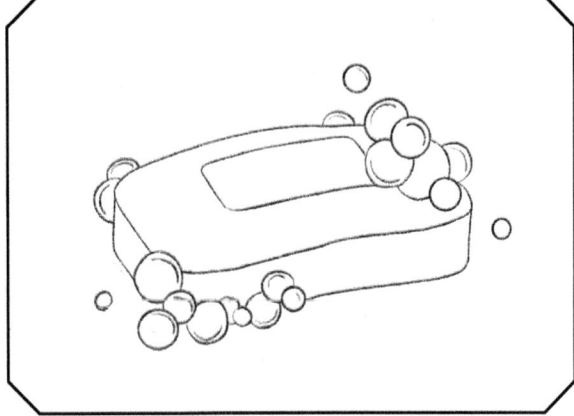

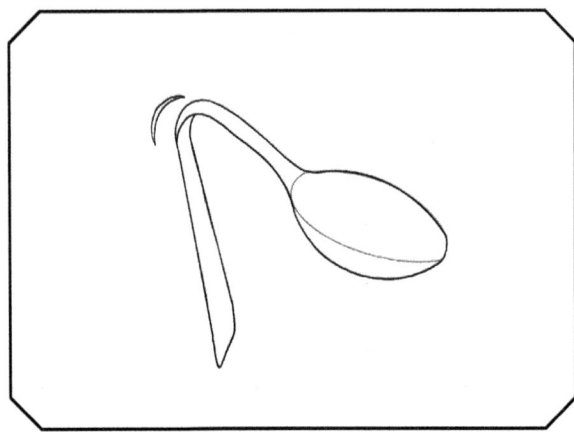

© Bloomsbury Education, 2026

'L' BLEND MINIMAL PAIRS CARDS

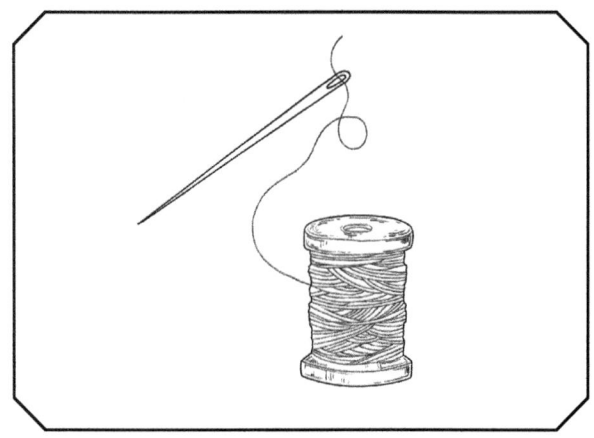
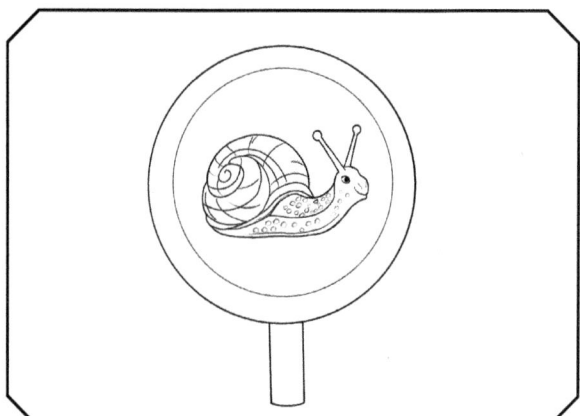

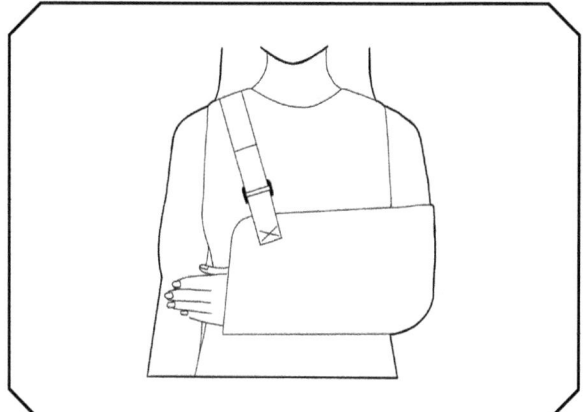

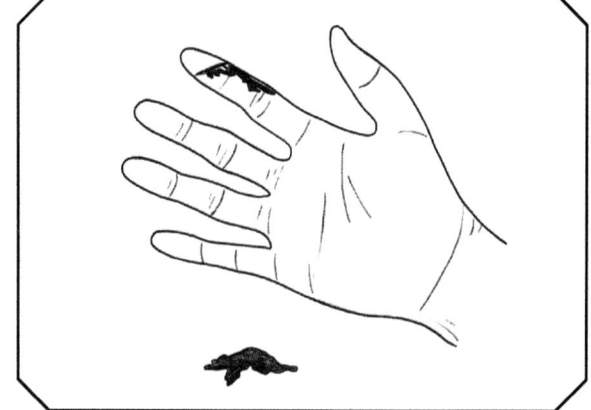

'L' BLEND MINIMAL PAIRS CARDS

'l' blend minimal pairs

back/black; cap/clap; soap/slope; bend/blend; kick/click; sew/slow; sing/sling; bud/blood; bow/blow; side/slide; pay/play; pain/plane

WHAT'S THE NEW WORD?

Week 27 say it	
Root word	+ sound
imp	l
eight	g
eat	f
aim	g
eel	f
am	j
at	m
ice	n
oat	b
or	f
ease	b
art	c

Week 28 say it	
Root word	+ blend
imp	bl
eight	pl
eat	sw
aim	cl
eel	st
am	sl
at	fl
ice	pr
oat	fl
or	st
ease	pl
art	sm

PEOPLE PICNIC GAME CARDS

Molly

Kai

Jake

Helen

© Bloomsbury Education, 2026

PEOPLE PICNIC GAME CARDS

Claire

Ellie

Fred

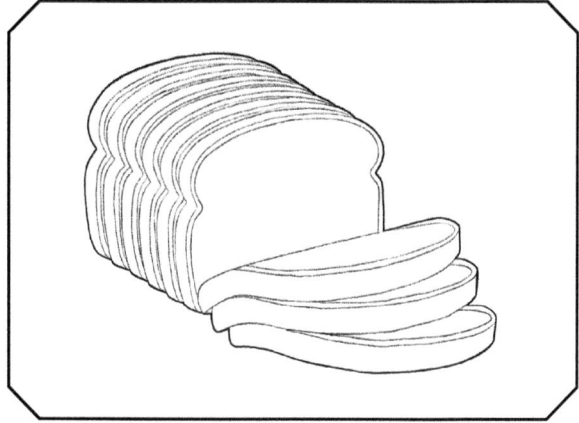

Betty

© Bloomsbury Education, 2026

RESOURCE 35

PEOPLE PICNIC GAME CARDS

Louise

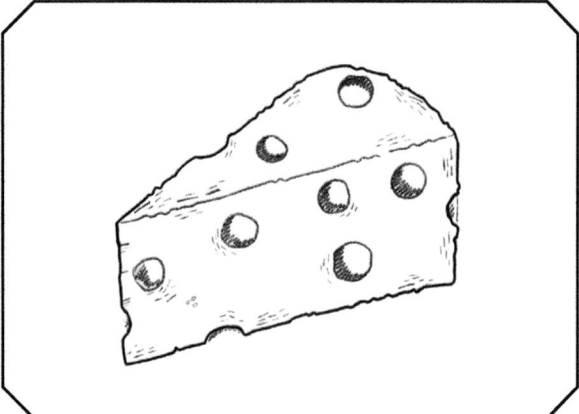

Meg

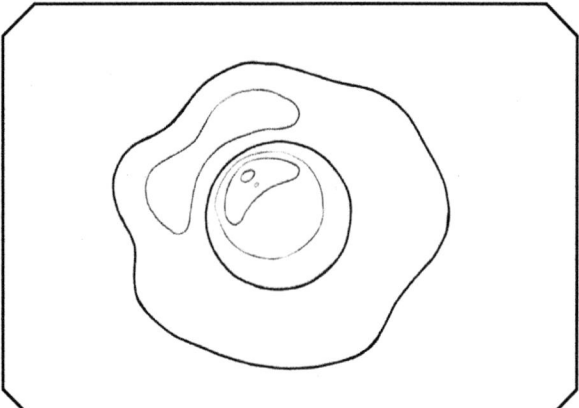

Luna

Lola

© Bloomsbury Education, 2026

'S' BLEND MINIMAL PAIRS CARDS

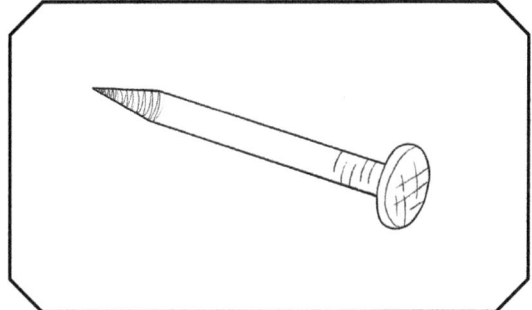
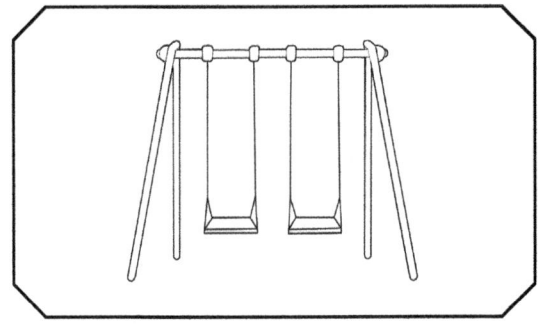

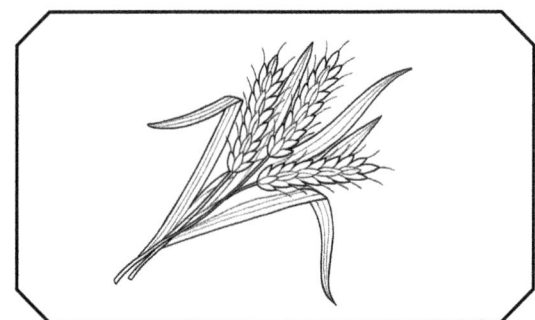

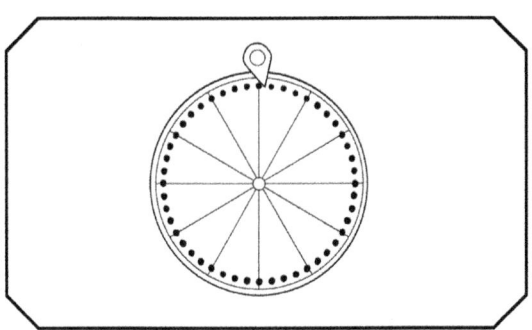

'S' BLEND MINIMAL PAIRS CARDS

Word list:

snail/nail; swing/wing; sweet/wheat; snow/no; spin/bin; spell/bell; spear/beer; slow/low; sneeze/knees; switch/witch

ADD A SYLLABLE, MAKE A WORD

| don | |
| mon |  |

| do | |
| pri |  |

| be | 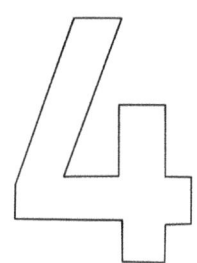 |

| ru | |
| ba |  |

| fu | |
| me |  |

ADD A SYLLABLE, MAKE A WORD

bo	
ro ca	
de a	
ye be he	
hu su fu	

FINAL BLEND MINIMAL PAIRS CARDS

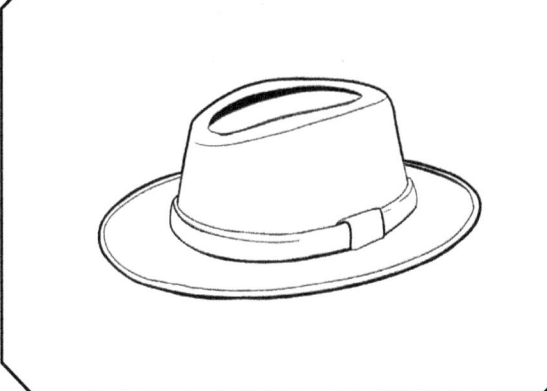

FINAL BLEND MINIMAL PAIRS CARDS

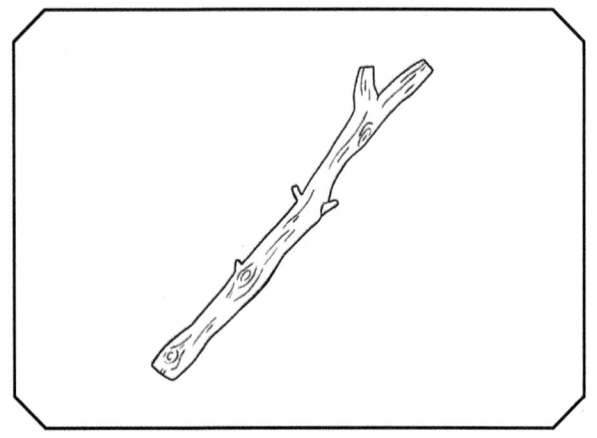

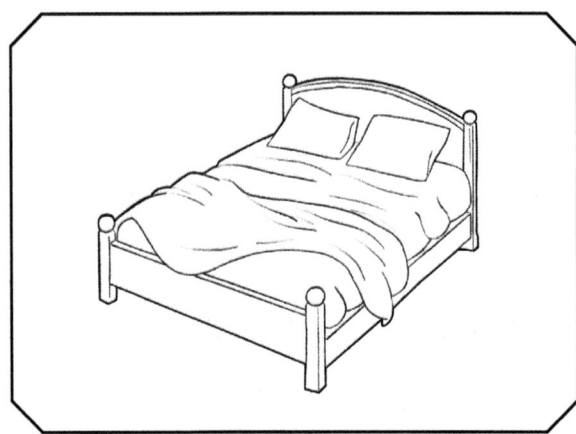

FINAL BLEND MINIMAL PAIRS CARDS

Word list:

net/nest; hut/hunt; cap/camp; vet/vest; stick/stink; plait/plant; goat/ghost; bed/bend; swap/swamp; lap/lamp; back/bank; black/blank

ANCHOR WORDS

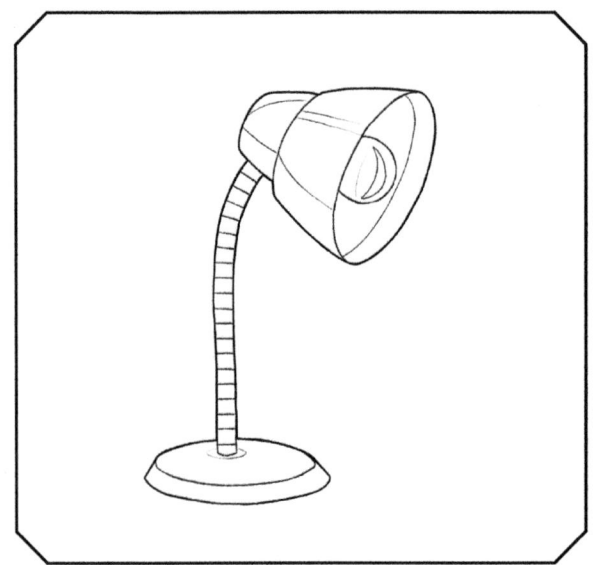

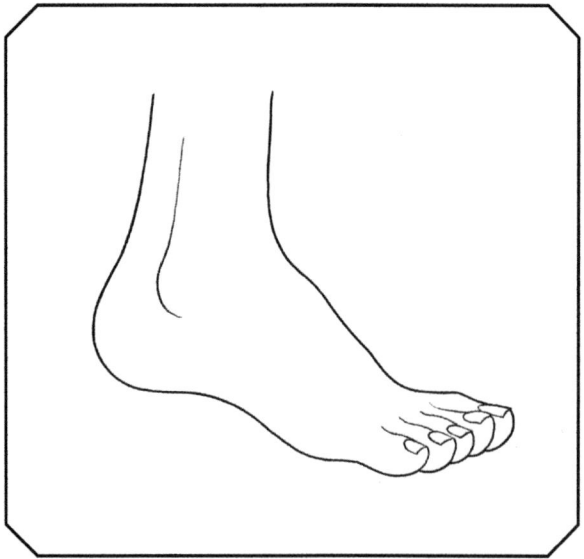

ANCHOR WORDS

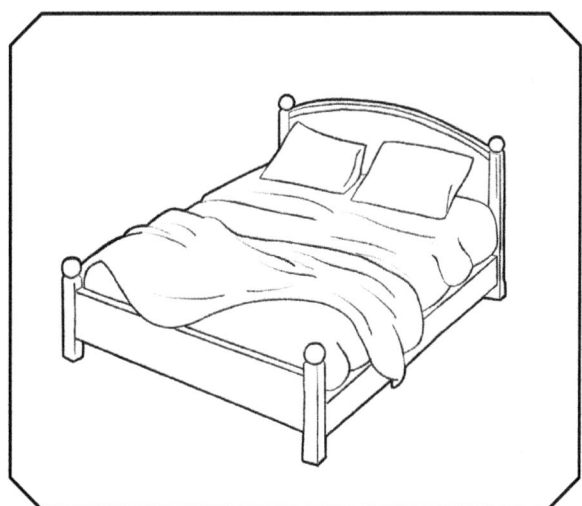

Anchor words

light   flower   fire   star   horse   foot   fish   car   sun   bed   sand   house

RESOURCE 39

ANCHOR WORDS: STEP DOWN CLUES

Anchor word	Possible words	Clues:
light	Lighthouse	A building by the sea
	Lightswitch	Turns a lamp on and off
	Lightbulb	Goes inside a lamp to make it work
flower	Sunflower	A tall yellow flower
	Flowerpot	A container for a plant
	Flowerbed	A somewhere in the garden where lots of plants grow
fire	Fireman	Someone who puts out fires
	Firework	You can see these in the sky on Bonfire night
	Firefly	A little insect that makes light
star	Starfish	A creature you find on the beach
	Starship	A vehicle that goes into space
	rockstar	A famous musician or singer
horse	Horseshoe	Something to protect a horse's hoof
	Seahorse	A creature that lives underwater
	Horsebox	A container to transport horses
foot	Football	A game with goals and two teams
	Snowball	Something you can make to play with when it snows
	Footstep	The noise you can hear when someone walks along
fish	Fishfinger	Something you can eat with chips
	Jellyfish	A creature with tentacles that lives under the sea
	Fishtank	A container with water for a pet
car	Car-key	You use this to open a vehicle door
	Carpark	A place for lots of vehicles
	Carwash	Somewhere to make vehicles clean
sun	Sunflower	A tall yellow flower
	Sunbed	Something to lie on by a swimming pool
	Sunhat	You put this on your head when it's hot
bed	Bunkbed	Two places to sleep in on top of each other
	Sunbed	Something to lie on by a swimming pool
	Flowerbed	Somewhere in the garden where lots of plants grow
sand	Sandcastle	A building you make on the beach
	Sandtray	A container of sand with toys in
	Sandwich	Something to eat with two slices of bread
house	Lighthouse	A building by the sea
	Houseboat	A home to live in on a river
	Greenhouse	A glass building where plants grow

© Bloomsbury Education, 2026

FINAL BLEND WORD LIST (CVCC WORDS)

best

vest

desk

pest

last

lost

cost

fast

mask

nest

list

dust

fist

bank

rank

lamp

pump

tent

went

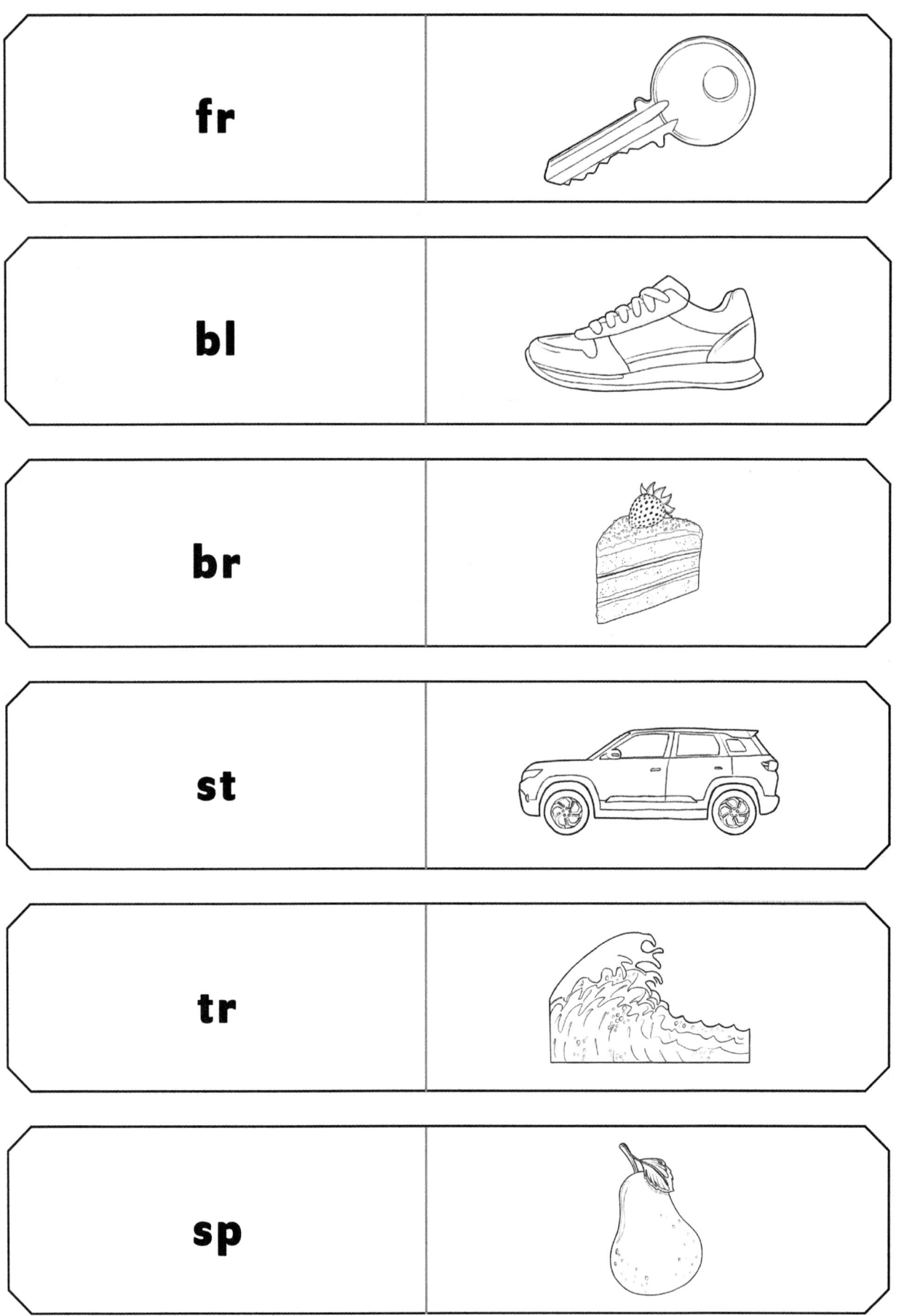

RHYME WORKSHOP CARDS

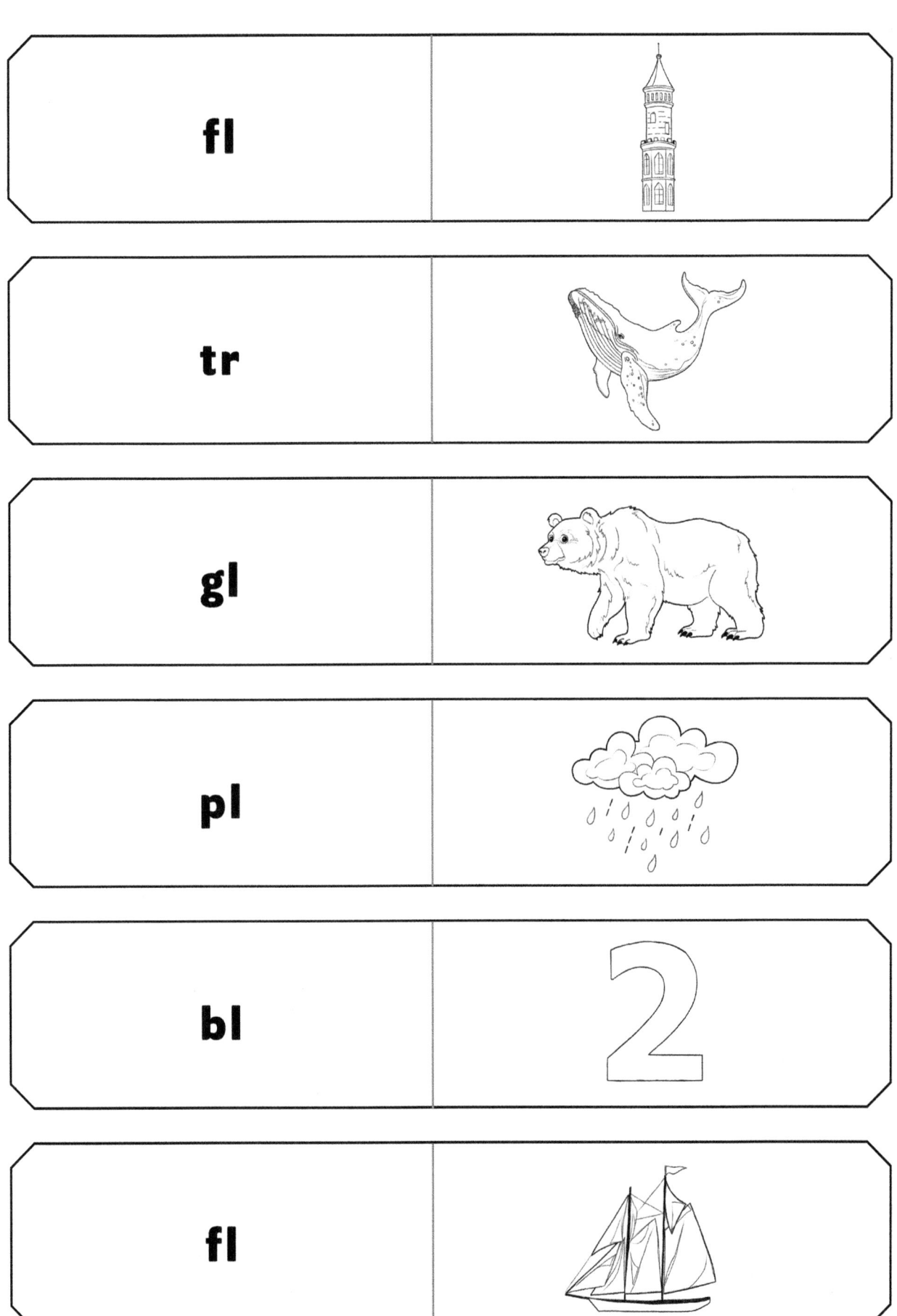

CATCH ME DOING IT!

I am trying to remember to use my ___ sound. Tick off a star every time you catch me remembering!

My reward will be:

CONSONANT BLENDS

bl	pl	sw
cl	st	sl
fl	pr	sm

References

McFaul, H., Mulgrew, L., Smyth, J. and Titterington, J. (2022), 'Applying evidence to practice by increasing intensity of intervention for children with severe speech sound disorder: a quality improvement project'. *BMJ Open Quality* 2022;11:e001761. doi: 10.1136/bmjoq-2021-001761

McCleod, S. and Crowe, K. (2018), 'Children's consonant acquisition in 27 language: A cross-linguistic review'. *American Journal of Speech-language Pathology*, 27, 1546-1571. doi: 101044/2018_AJSLP-17-0100

Stackhouse, J. & Wells, B. (1997), *Children's Speech and Literacy Difficulties: A psycholinguistic framework*. London: Whurr Publishers.